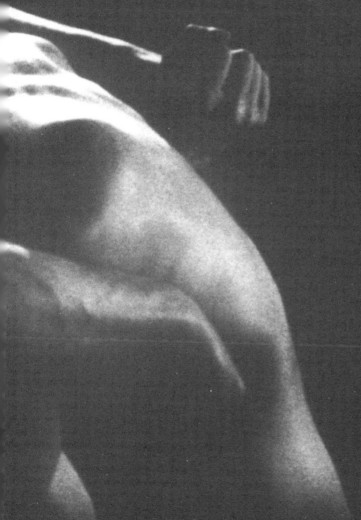

The Cinema of
Jean Genet

The Cinema of
Jean Genet
Un Chant d'amour

JANE GILES

BFI Publishing

First published in 1991 by the
British Film Institute
21 Stephen Street, London W1P 1PL

Reprinted 1992

Frontispiece: photo of Jean Genet by Brassaï
Inside front and inside back cover: *Un Chant d'amour*

British Library Cataloguing in Publication Data
Giles, Jane *1964–*
    The Cinema of Jean Genet : Un Chant d'amour.
    1. French Cinema films. Production
    I. Title II. Un Chant d'amour
791.4302320944

ISBN 0–85170–289–9

Designed by Stella Crew, 2D Design
Typeset by Fakenham Photosetting Limited,
Fakenham, Norfolk
and printed in Great Britain by
The Trinity Press, Worcester, and London

Contents

Acknowledgments

The author wishes to thank the following for their co-operation in preparing this book:

Claude Autant-Lara, Stephen Barber, Stuart Burleigh, Gavin Bryars, Collectif Jeune Cinéma/Jean-Paul Dupuis, Elizabeth Cowie/University of Kent, Albert Dichy, Derek Jarman, Richard Kwietniowski, Jonas Mekas, Nico Papatakis, Tony Rayns, Paule Thévenin and Edmund White.

Stills by courtesy of BFI Stills, Posters and Designs and BFI Distribution Division.

Thanks to Roma Gibson, BFI Publishing Services.

Jean Genet was interested in the cinema from the very beginning of his career as a writer. Whereas Jean-Paul Sartre postulates that Genet progressed from the solipsism of lyric poetry to progressively more social (and socially concerned) forms of fiction, drama and film, in fact as early as 1942 Genet had already completed not only his long poem *The Man Condemned to Death*, but also his novel *Our Lady of the Flowers* and a first draft of *Death Watch* (called *Pour la belle*) and was hoping to direct a film.

Indeed, a close look at the composition of his novels reveals that he was profoundly influenced by the cinematic techniques of collage, flashback, and close-up. Just as *Un Chant d'amour*, as Jane Giles explains, intercuts the warder's sexual fantasies with realistic scenes of the prisoners in their cell as well as one prisoner's daydream of a woodland erotic romp, in the same way each of the five novels juxtaposes two or three separate plots. For instance, in *Our Lady of the Flowers*, Divine's present life in Montmartre as a transvestite prostitute is intercalated with scenes of his life as the boy Culafroy in a village as well as with scenes of Our Lady's crimes and trial. In a characteristically cinematic rearrangement of sequence, the novel begins with Divine's death and interment, then leads us through his life and hundreds of pages back to this conclusion.

Close-ups of gestures are also essential to Genet's conception of the novel, since in his ontology accidents determine fate, gestures form character and costume triggers events. As Jane Giles quotes from a Genet film script, 'In effect the cinema is basically immodest. Let us use this faculty to enlarge gestures. The cinema can open a fly and search out its secrets....'

Un Chant d'amour, the only film Genet both wrote and directed, reveals in a pure form the techniques he adopted to fiction and the theatre, a subject Giles discusses with acuity and convincing detail. In addition this film shows his lyric vision of homosexual love, at once highly physical and romantic. Like the photographer Robert Mapplethorpe, who knew of Genet through the singer Patti Smith, Genet presents acts of homosexual love in a light that seems at once offensive to the naive and ennobling to the initiated. Neither Genet nor Mapplethorpe, however, could be considered sexually stimulating, since both make abstractions out of the male body.

Indeed Genet never completely resolved, even in his own mind, to what degree his writing was pornographic. His first novel, *Our Lady of the Flowers*, was originally published in 1943 in a limited deluxe edition intended primarily for the homosexual market. When the same text was later reprinted by Gallimard for the general public, Genet himself removed many shocking details (such as the dimensions of the characters' penises). Many years later he was capable of asking a friend if he regarded his work as mere pornography.

Genet maintained an unstable relationship with all of his work. For instance, he did not let Nico Papatakis make a film out of his one-act play *The Maids* because one of his woman friends had convinced him the text was badly 'dated', although he endorsed Papatakis' filmed version of the original real-life murder and trial that had inspired the play (Giles reprints Genet's statement in praise of Papatakis' *Les Abysses*).

Similarly, Genet was certain his poetry was valueless and constantly asked friends if they thought his fiction would live. He disliked the end of *The Balcony* and long after *The Screens* was premiered he was still tinkering with the script.

His rejection of *Un Chant d'amour* may have had its roots in his fear that it, too, was botched or that it was merely pornographic. Certainly by the time he denounced it definitively in the 1970s he had written several other film scripts, as Giles' chronology indicates, and his ideas about cinema as an art had evolved. Perhaps he feared the short early film would be considered amateurish and would compromise his chances to find funding for new projects (some of these projects could be extravagant, as the late scenarios reveal). In the case of *La Nuit venue* Genet worked with a collaborator on a full-length fiction scenario over a long period and through several drafts, only to block the production himself when everything was ready to go.

The curious thing is that Genet thought about cinema early and late throughout his long writing career. In fact he wrote more pages of film scenarios than he did any other literary genre. But *Un Chant d'amour* is the only testimony we have of what his real cinematic taste and style might render.

To some extent it may be seen as a response to Cocteau. In 1943 Genet had been discovered and launched by Cocteau, who arranged for *Our Lady of the Flowers* to be published, and who circulated the manuscript among many important Parisian writers and taste-makers. In the 1940s Cocteau, who was living with film actor Jean Marais, was involved with many major film projects, including most notably his post-war international success, *La Belle et la bête*. Genet watched Cocteau's activity with a mixture of envy, admiration and irritation. Indeed in the early 1950s Genet, assuming what Cocteau called a 'Jansenist' stance, denounced Cocteau for his disgusting involvement with the 'industrial cinema'. Could it be that *Un Chant d'amour*, which was partially shot at Cocteau's country house at Milly-la-Forêt, might be seen both as an echo of Cocteau's mythic, magical cinema and as a criticism of its crowd-pleasing use of linear narration, traditional plot and famous actors?

As the sole realisation of Genet's persistent love of the movies, *Un Chant d'amour* is an unclaimed pledge in the vast pawn shop of his imagination. Jane Giles has provided us with everything we need to know about this brilliant missed chance.

Edmund **White**

'Tough and sure, both a weapon of liberation and a love poem.'

Jean Genet/Introduction to *Soledad Brother*[1]

Written and directed by Jean Genet in 1950, the short film *Un Chant d'amour* now exists as a shard in his oeuvre of published poems, plays and novels. Genet had maintained an antagonistic attitude towards the public consumption of his work, and was always caught between capitalising upon his literary abilities and having an outsider's resistance to the social and cultural reintegration which would inevitably follow from his works' availability and popularity. But Genet's opposition to the public exhibition of *Un Chant d'amour*, his only fully realised film project, was consistent and exceptionally vitriolic.

Un Chant d'amour was made shrouded in the anonymity of pornography, and was intended for the eyes of private collectors only. Yet it has regularly demonstrated the ability of a film to elude the absolute control of its maker in a way unlike that of any other medium, to become 'the most famous gay short film in European history'[2]. The negative exists safely vaulted away in the name of its producer, who owns the rights to the film in return for his original financial input. Genet partially succeeded in delimiting the exhibition of *Un Chant d'amour* in France, but its producer had already sold a number of prints abroad to independent film distributors. From these the film had a limited availability on the 'underground' cinema circuit, although the opportunities to see it were even further reduced by its periodic censorship and the prosecution of its exhibitors under the problematic obscenity laws.

In addition to the historically limited availability of *Un Chant d'amour*, it is made inaccessible both by the medium of film itself, which demands the specific apparatus of projector and screen in darkness in order to be seen, and by Genet's construction of narrative content. Pared down to an intense twenty-five minutes, *Un Chant d'amour* densely intercuts three strands of a story with the effect on first viewing of a confusion of time, space and character, an effect which has undoubtedly exasperated and antagonised those already hostile to the film's sexually explicit material, and seeking censorship.

The intention of this book is to counteract the suppression and subsequent silence and confusion which have surrounded *Un Chant d'amour* since its inception. By making the production context and exhibition histories available, and by giving a shot-by-shot description of the film's content, the aim is to show the relevance of this unique filmic rendition by Genet of his ideas, and to celebrate the presence of *Un Chant d'amour* in his oeuvre, which although primarily one of literature and drama, by no means ever excluded the possibilities of the medium of film.

Notes

1. Introduction to *Soledad Brother* by George Jackson (London: Jonathan Cape, 1971).
2. Tony Rayns, letter to the author, 28 July 1986.

Genet and Film¹

While *Un Chant d'amour* remained his only fully realised film, Jean Genet (1910–86) was a cinematic flirt and worked on several other projects, including scripts written at a time later in his life when he was publicly assumed to have been least productive. Nico Papatakis, Genet's one time accomplice and the producer of *Un Chant d'amour*, believes that Genet never intended these scripts to be realised in celluloid images, and that he probably found this a way of obtaining financial advances without making a final commitment. However, at least two of these scripts seem to have reached the advanced stage of pre-production, and furthermore when Genet objected to the recognition awarded to *Un Chant d'amour* in 1975 by the Centre Nationale de la Cinématographie, one of his grounds was that the film should not be prized as if it were the most recent fulfilment of his work. Both these points suggest that Genet did not completely abandon the prospect of visualising his written ideas onto film.

The Scripts

La Révolte des anges noirs, 1947
(The Revolt of the Black Angels)

According to *La Presse Magazine* in June 1947, Genet was working on a biographical film script based on his childhood and entitled *La Révolte des anges noirs*. It was unrealised as a film.

Le Prisonnier, 1949 (The Prisoner)

In the 1940s, Genet agreed to write the dialogue for Pierre Chenal and Roger Vailland's film *Le Prisonnier*, an adaptation of Hans Fallada's 1937 novel, *Le Roman du prisonnier*. Genet apparently received a cheque for between twenty and twenty-five million old French francs in advance from the producer, but the project was grounded and Genet may never have started writing the explicit and specific prison slang dialogue commissioned from him.[2]

Le Bagne, 1950s (The Penal Colony)

Following the successful production of *Un Chant d'amour* in 1950, Genet produced a 133-page script, *Le Bagne*. In 1952 *Paris-Presse* reported Genet's work on the film script, and indicated that shooting would begin the following year in Rome. In 1955 the journal *Carrefour* announced the completion of the script and the news that the twenty-year-old actor Pierre Joly, a young Marlon Brando look-alike, would take a leading role. The script is highly developed, and includes notes on camera direction (see Appendix II) and casting (for example, the character of the penal colony director is described as physically resembling the actor Charles Laughton).

Un Chant d'amour was not made as a pilot for *Le Bagne*. However, there are similarities between ideas and images established in the short completed film and the unrealised script, which Genet described as a 'drame pédérastique', taking place in a penal colony in a desert reminiscent of French Guyana or Devil's Island. In addition to both being focused on a prison, its inmates and its keepers, *Le Bagne* repeats and enlarges upon the structure of a series of cells, picturing twenty-three, each containing a different tableau or spectacle (prisoners smoke, dance, lie on the bed and so on). The cells are linked by Le Bagnard's dialogue, rather than the warder's intrusive eye, as in *Un*

Chant d'amour. Furthermore, *Le Bagne* presents an elaboration of the recurrent image of the warder's eye peeping through the spyhole of the cell door. In both films the prisoner becomes aware of the warder's presence, but with radically different reactions. In *Un Chant d'amour* the inmate merely smiles, although his recognition of the warder's presence is signalled by a 'crisis' in the film as the shot of the warder's eye looking through the spyhole is edited in upside-down. In *Le Bagne* the convict approaches the door, exhaling cigarette smoke to conceal his proximity, and plunges a needle through the spyhole into the eye of the warder, causing his death. This image was used again by Genet more than twenty years later in his final film script, *Le Langage de la muraille* (The Language of the Walls).

Le Bagne was never made, and at Sotheby's auction in London, November 1988, bidding for the film script failed to reach the reserve price of £8,000. Included in the lot were one hundred and sixty pages of notes and drawings by Genet for an also unrealised stage play of *Le Bagne*.

Les Rêves interdits, ou L'autre versant du rêve, c. 1952 (Forbidden Dreams or The Other Side of Dreams)

Genet presented his 103-page film script *Les Reves interdits, ou L'autre versant du rêve* to the actress Anouk Aimée on her marriage to Nico Papatakis in 1952, but later sold the rights to the script three times without telling her. In an English version by Bernard Frechtman (who translated most of Genet's novels and plays), *Les Rêves interdits* became the basis of Tony Richardson's film *Mademoiselle* made in 1966, starring Jeanne Moreau, a stage actress favoured by Genet, and later to feature in Fassbinder's adaptation of *Querelle de Brest* (Querelle of Brest, 1947). Genet receives the sole screen credit for the script, which centres upon a small French village plagued by fires and poisoned water supplies. The villagers believe that a group of immigrant Italian woodcutters are responsible for the destruction, while the real culprit is 'Mademoiselle', a prim schoolteacher who disguises her night of passion with one of the Italian workers as a rape, with fatal consequences.

La Nuit venue/Le Bleu de l'oeil, 1976–78
(The Night Has Come/The Blue of the Eye)

Collaborating with Ghislain Uhry and the producer Claude Nedjar, Genet's script *Le Bleu de l'oeil*, later titled *La Nuit venue*, reached the advanced stage of pre-production and a budget of five million francs; by early 1977 Genet had received an advance for this film which was to be shot in the summer of that year, although the project was never finally realised.

Stylistically, the film bears a greater resemblance to Genet's play *Les Paravents* (The Screens, 1961) than to *Un Chant d'amour* or any of his prison-based literature. The snatch of the script that has been published demonstrates a powerful consciousness of colour (both racial and literal), the use of flashbacks, the settings of hospitals, brothels and market places and bizarre, highly exaggerated costumes:

> *In the distance there are silhouettes; two or three are dressed as women – one with a parasol and train, despite the night. The women are much bigger than the men ... The white cop and the Black are bigger than life (nearly on stilts). The face and hands of the Black are golden ... It's a circus scene where the nurses play a game with the beds on wheels ... Costumes of the arab workers in the line: black – a lot of black – green, yellow – indigo blue ... Transvestites all along the stairway.*[3]

Le Langage de la muraille: cent ans jour après jour, 1970s
(The Language of the Walls: One Hundred Years Day after Day)

Genet's last film script project was a semi-fiction/semi-documentary account of the borstal at Mettray where he spent his adolescence incarcerated. For Genet, Mettray was paradoxically both a place of deprivation and punitive horror, and an abundant haven of fraternity and eroticism – a 'family' made up of hundreds of brothers. *Le Langage de la muraille* seems to be a project more closely related to his pre-1950 work with literature and film: *Un Chant d'amour* also has a visual style that is partly realist and partly imaginary, seen in the difference between the sequences set in the jail and those of the warder's erotic fantasies. The film is structured around the importance of the cell wall, as the object which both withholds and therefore maintains desire. *Le Langage de la muraille* features the 'needle in the eye' image which is first described in *Le Bagne*.

Literature and Film

Genet's novels bear occasional references to the cinema (in both literal and metaphoric terms), and an awareness of other media which works as both an extra dimension in his writing and a suggestion of the possibilities of other formats. For example, in *Pompes funèbres* (Funeral Rites, 1947), there is a long description of going to see a military-type movie and the viewer (Genet) elaborating erotically upon the given story. In the novel *Miracle de la rose* (Miracle of the Rose, 1945–6) Genet writes:

> *I had not got over the horror I felt, when I was arrested, of suddenly being a character in a film who is involved in a drama of which the agonising outcome is unknown since it may reach just the point at*

*which the reel is cut or burned, and so make me
disappear in the darkness or the fire, dead before my
death.*[4]

This poetic comparison predicted the fate of Genet's own
print of *Un Chant d'amour*. It was entrusted to the Cinémathèque
Française where it was destroyed in a nitrate fire in 1980.

The Adaptations

Several of Genet's plays and novels have been adapted by
others as feature films: *The Balcony* (Joseph Strick, 1962) from the
1957 play *Le Balcon; Arrestation d'un tireur des toits* (Pierre Grimblat,
1962) from *Pompes Funèbres; Deathwatch* (Vic Morrow, 1965) from
the 1949 play *Haute Surveillance; The Maids* (Christopher Miles,
1974) from the 1947 play *Les Bonnes; Querelle – Ein pakt mit dem
Teufel (Querelle)* (Rainer Werner Fassbinder, 1981) from the novel
Querelle de Brest.

The Maids

Querelle

Fassbinder's savagely beautiful film is both an imaginative and respectful adaptation of Genet's novel, paying homage to the original medium by incorporating sections of the black hand-written word coming out of a blinding white page between the lustrous gold and blue images. Acquiring the film rights to the book from the by then self-exiled Genet was a formidable achievement for Dieter Schidor, the producer of *Querelle*, which he described in an interview of 1981:

> [*Genet*] *didn't have a fixed abode. Then I found out that he lived in Essen, but had moved to Beirut after the Palestinian massacres and he's still there. He's still a revolutionary. He went to support the Palestinians. Everyone is surprised that he finally gave the rights. There must have been a combination of reasons for Genet at that moment, not the least of which was financial, because he got nearly $100,000. He supports many people. He is very generous and there are people who depend on him. Not that he is anywhere near poor, but it is also nice to have an extra $100,000. Of course, people have been trying to get the rights for many years. We exchanged letters and maybe he trusted my naive way. Maybe he felt a kind of private energy from me, that I wanted to do this special film, not just any film.*[5]

To one of the letters Schidor wrote to Genet during the film's pre-production, he received the reply that the novel had been written a long time ago, suggesting both that Genet had forgotten the plot (he did not re-read his past work and he was long addicted to memory-affecting nembutal) and that his interest lay in projects of the present and future. Genet's letter to Schidor is reproduced as the last image of *Querelle*.

In 1962 Nico Papatakis completed his directorial debut, *Les Abysses* (The Depths). It was not adapted from Genet's play *Les Bonnes*, but was based on the same source material, the Papin sisters murder case, and uses in microcosm the themes of humiliation and revolution. The film caused some officials and critics to riot at the Cannes Film Festival, as they thought that *Les Abysses* brought French film-making into disrepute, and that it should not have been chosen as part of the Official Selection. Papatakis fuelled the controversy by graphically describing his brutal working method, which reduced the two actresses (Francine and Colette Berge, both ballet dancers) to a state of nervous collapse, as he refused to let them wash and constantly encouraged them to fight, until they ended up by hitting him ('... which was just what I wanted', Papatakis is reported to have said). The script of *Les Abysses* was written by Jean Vauthier and the film was publicly renowned by Jean-Paul Sartre; Simone de Beauvoir; André Breton; Jacques Prévert and Genet. Genet's review of the film was entitled 'From Beginning to End, a Tornado':

> *'All the sorrow of the world' ... the famous phrase could also describe the tornado from beginning to end that is* Les Abysses. *One would have to be deaf not to distinguish the weak but precious wail through the growling of the girls about to be pulled out of their slow degradation against their will. The two sisters (only they count in the film) are first seen next to a fire – and already bitten by it. It would be understandable if one cried out against the tenacity with which Nico Papatakis has been able to seize and lead this paroxysm for two hours. But I think one should keep one's eyes wide open when an acrobat executes a deadly performance.*[6]

In 1989 Papatakis was known to have been researching the art of the tightrope walker, and so it is possible that his next film project will be an adaptation of Genet's monograph, *La Funambule*.

Film Appearances by Genet

Genet is reported to be seen in Alexandre Astruc's *Ulysse, ou les mauvaises rencontres*, shot in and around the bars of Saint Germain des Prés in 1948.

In 1950 he made a three-minute long home movie, horsing around with the author Violette Leduc – she plays a mother and Genet her baby.

Documentary footage of Genet at the 1968 Chicago Democratic Convention is used in Robin Spry's film, *Prologue* (Canada, 1969), a fictionalised study of the dilemma of activism.

Antoine Bourseiller conducted a series of interviews which comprise his documentary film *Genet* (France, 1981). Contributions are also made by the actor and theatrical director of Genet's plays, Roger Blin, and by the artist Alberto Giacometti, who was the subject of Genet's monograph *L'Atelier d'Alberto Giacometti* and who painted the famous portrait of Genet in 1955.

Genet refused to give interviews for several years, but in 1985 came to London to be filmed over two days by the BBC for an *Arena* documentary, *Saint Genet*. For this he demanded £10,000 in advance ('like a whore' commented Edmund White in his obituary of Genet in *The Literary Review*, September 1986). Chain-smoking Gitanes with yellow fingers and dressed in surprisingly modern casual clothes, Genet gave the BBC a feisty, value-for-money interview. He quite literally turns the cameras around onto his questioners (whom Genet accuses of behaving like the police) and directly addresses the film's reluctant technicians, asking them why they don't revolt against their lack of rights to speak and push him out of the picture (phrasing this fantasy/idea as a dream from the previous night). This was Genet's last appearance on, and involvement with, film. He died in April 1986.

Notes

1. See also Appendix IV.
2. Alain and Odette Virmaux, 'Genet, Vaillant, Chenal', *Cinématographe* no. 122, September 1986.
3. See Appendix III.
4. *Miracle of the Rose* (London: Anthony Blond, 1965), p. 101.
5. Gregory Solman, 'The Wizard of Babylon: An Interview with Dieter Schidor', *Cinéaste*, vol. 13, no. 1, 1983, pp. 40–42.
6. Included in press notes issued in 1963 for UK release of *Les Abysses*.

So while cinema is a consistent strand in Genet's work, *Un Chant d'amour*, made in 1950, exists as the only filmic example of his transposition of ideas and writing into images.

Synopsis

Approaching a prison, a Warder's eye is caught by the strange sight of a bouquet of blossom being repeatedly swung from one barred cell window to another, each time failing to be grasped by an emerging hand. He goes to investigate, and peeping into a series of cells sees in each one a male prisoner masturbating. The Warder's excited eye becomes fixed on the mute dialogue between an agitated North African prisoner and his neighbour, a young, disinterested, tattooed convict. They communicate via the constraining cell wall, which in itself becomes the object of desire, tattooed and tearful, to be caressed, kissed, punched and pierced. The two men erotically exchange cigarette smoke through a straw in a hole in the wall. This sight fires the Warder's chiaroscuro-lit fantasies of fucking another man, signalled by a hand reaching for swinging white blossom. Disturbed, the Warder enters the older prisoner's cell and brutally thrashes him, initiating the prisoner's own daydream of a woodland romance with the young convict, who holds blossom in front of his fly. The Warder leaves the cell, but returns to insert his gun into the mouth of the older prisoner.

The Warder leaves the prison, but looking back over his shoulder once again sees the relentlessly swinging bouquet of blossom. He walks away and so doesn't see that the flowers are finally caught.

Production

Towards the end of the Second World War Genet met Nico Papatakis (b. 1918 in Addis Ababa), an enigmatic blue-eyed Greek who was then the owner of an innovative cabaret nightclub called La Rose Rouge, situated in the Rue des Rennes in Saint Germain des Prés and popular with the Existentialists. Papatakis discovered and featured artistes such as Juliet Greco and Les Frères Jacques, and as Jean Cau, Jean-Paul Sartre's secretary, later said, the club was 'LE lieu nocturne des belles années'. Genet was attracted to the handsome and violent Papatakis (who was also described as 'the idlest of Paris playboys') and the two became accomplices. Soon after his release from an intended life sentence after thirteen convictions for petty theft and one for desertion (Jean Cocteau and Sartre petitioned Vincent Auriol, then President of France, who granted the pardon), Genet proposed the idea of making an erotic film to Papatakis, who agreed to put up the money. Papatakis budgeted for a silent black and white film up to an hour in length, shot on 16mm – the experimental, porn and home movie format of that time. Papatakis also gave the empty space above La Rose Rouge in which to build the film's prison sets. The woodland sequences in *Un Chant d'amour* were filmed in the forest of Milly, south of Paris, which was the home of Cocteau, who apparently came to watch the filming. The exterior stone wall seen at the very beginning and end of the film belonged to Genet's former prison, La Sante, where he wrote the predominantly biographical novel, *Miracle de la rose*, and was filmed without the necessary permission of the authorities.

To render *Un Chant d'amour* technically perfect, the crew hired were all professionals, and included the cinematographer Jacques Natteau, who had shot *La Bête humaine* (Jean Renoir, 1938) and who later worked with the film directors Marcel Carné, Jules Dassin, and most prolifically with Claude Autant-Lara.[1]

On the other hand, none of the cast were professional actors, with the exception of André Reybaz. Reybaz had appeared in a number of films and plays, and later became a theatre director. He had a small part in *Un Chant d'amour*, appearing from the waist down as a stand-in for the more modest leading actor. The men in the film were chosen by Genet from his circle of Montmartre mates and cronies. The character of the younger convict with the tattoo is played by Lucien (Marius) Sénemaud who had been in the army with Cocteau's lover and leading man Jean Marais, through whom he met Genet. Sénemaud became Genet's lover and accomplice, and is named in his novel *Journal du voleur* (The Thief's Journal, 1949) and characterised as 'Maurice' in his play *Haute Surveillance*. Genet adored Sénemaud, setting him up with a house and business in Le Cannet, and with a wife, Ginette, whose son from a previous marriage, Jackie Maglia, later also became Genet's lover. Genet wanted to call the Sénemauds' house 'Maison des Voleurs' (House of Thieves) but Ginette found this to be a little too close to the bone. Genet kept his own room with them, and Lucien still works as a mechanic at his 'Garage Saint-Genet'. Genet dedicated *Haute Surveillance* and the poems 'Le Pecheur du Suquet' (The Fisherman of Suquet) and 'Un Chant d'amour' (A Song of Love) to Lucien Sénemaud. The poem 'Un Chant d'amour' was published in 1950, but apart from the title, date, the connection with Sénemaud, and a certain bucolic emphasis, it bears little resemblance to the film. Lucien missed the birth of his first child, Robert, on 21 April 1950 because he was in Paris filming *Un Chant d'amour* for fifteen days from 8 April. Despite this division of her husband's loyalties, Ginette is positive about the film; she and Lucien first saw it in Antibes and she jokes that Lucien likes *Un Chant d'amour* 'because he's in it!' whilst Lucien has nothing to say on the matter.[2] The hand that swings the bouquet of blossom at the beginning and end of *Un Chant d'amour* belongs to Java, who like Lucien was also one of Genet's lovers and criminal accomplices, and is featured in *Journal du voleur*. He was another friend set up in a legitimate business by Genet – this time running a dry cleaning shop in the mid-South of France.

The character of the black prisoner who performs an erotic dance in *Un Chant d'amour* was played by a professional dancer who worked in the cabarets of Montmartre and whose stage name was 'Coco Le Martiniquais'. He recalls the character of Clément Village, the narrator's cell mate in Genet's novel *Notre Dame des Fleurs* (Our Lady of the Flowers, 1944). Village is described as being a one time nude dancer at the 'Viennese Dreamland' – a pimp who had murdered his girl, and was later killed during the jailbreak at Cayennes.

The character of the older prisoner was played by a North African pimp who also worked as a barber in Montmartre.

None of the cast or crew have their names credited on the film. Papatakis claims that this was necessary to avoid the persecutions and stigma of the film's socially perceived pornographic status. All members were paid off substantially, but, wary of blackmail, Papatakis is still unwilling to disclose their names. The only name credited on *Un Chant d'amour* is that of Genet himself, already outside of the law, establishing from the very first shot (the title 'UN CHANT D'AMOUR PAR JEAN GENET') that he is the 'auteur' of the film, a position which he was to reassert vigorously in print twenty-five years later. The last image of *Un Chant d'amour* shows a cell wall scored off with ten digits and the dates 'Avril–Juin 1950' (the period of the film's production) plus the initials 'M.A.V.' and 'B.A.A.D.C.'. These initials do not stand for the names of the leading actors or characters or technicians, but are also found in the novel *Miracle de la rose* as the common graffiti on convicts' cell walls which haunted Genet, and mean 'Mort aux vaches' (Death to the cops) and 'Bonjour aux amis du malheur' (Greetings to friends in misfortune).[3]

Some sources have erroneously credited Cocteau's name to the production of *Un Chant d'amour*. Nico Papatakis has stated that although Cocteau came to watch the shooting, he had no input nor influence (neither did Papatakis, other than his financial commitment). In an interview with André Fraigneau in 1951, Cocteau is asked whether Genet had made a film. He replies: 'Yes, a beautiful film in which [Genet] uses the visual language with the greatest ease. But it is very difficult to see that film.'[4]

The imagined affiliation of Cocteau with the production of *Un Chant d'amour* is probably inspired by the poetic style shared with his films. Jean Cau is certain that Genet's film was influenced by *Le Sang d'un poète* (Blood of a Poet) directed by Jean Cocteau in 1930 and feels hostile:

> *When you change genres, it's always terrifying, it obliges a change in one's entire artistic approach. Genet didn't realize that and you'll see all his metaphors laid bare. Sperm, splashing, becomes a rose – it's completely ridiculous. Genet thought it would be a revolutionary film. He didn't see how ridiculous it was.*[5]

Others have suggested that *Un Chant d'amour* was influenced by Kenneth Anger's *Fireworks* (1947) which Anger claims

Genet saw at the Cinémathèque Française in 1950. In a 1989 interview Anger was questioned about the relation between the two films, to which he replied:

> *I met Genet and he just shrugged his own movie off. The film was paid for by the owner of the Rose Rouge nightclub, Nico Papatakis, and so it had more production values. It was filmed on 35mm with a professional cameraman, so it certainly had a more slick look than my little film – but I think I did pretty good, with my hundred dollar budget.*[6]

After viewing the first 16mm rushes Genet and Natteau were disappointed with the quality, and so shooting began again in the professional 35mm format. The first rough edit (supervised by Genet) was forty-five minutes long, but dissatisfied with this, Genet immediately cut the film down to a concise twenty-five minutes which remains the definitive version. The film had cost the equivalent of about £20,000 today.

Genet and Papatakis did not submit *Un Chant d'amour* for the visa, certificate or rating necessary if the film was to be shown in commercial or public cinemas. Instead a number of prints were sold privately in an attempt to recoup the film's costs. The young American composer Ned Rorem describes in his *Paris Diary* seeing the film in such circumstances in 1953:

> *Finally saw Genet's movie. It was so much like everyone says that there's little surprise. (Jacob Wasserman's prison chapters were more remarkable but less pederast.) Creation is not based on experiences we've had, but on things we've imagined, woven,*

and finished; experiences we have not had. A great
writer has not the time to live himself ... Of course
the best scenes (which F[reddy] Reichenback pro-
jected on his wall, wrongly using Bartok for back-
ground) were not the out-and-out masturbation-
without-climax 'shots', but the smoke puffed into a
straw, breathed and reabsorbed through the hole in a
prison wall, from mouth to mouth by lovers who
cannot, haven't and will never see each other.[7]

In 1952 the former Surrealist Charles Henri Ford, who owned a copy of *Un Chant d'amour*, organised a private screening, attended by Genet, in order to try to sell the print to the artist Arturo Lopez. Lopez refused to buy the film, apparently scared that his servants would walk out on him if they ever saw it.

The practically 'unshowable' nature of *Un Chant d'amour* was anticipated by Jean Boullet in his review of the film for Eric Rohmer's *Gazette du Cinéma* in September 1950. While praising the poetic beauty and strength of *Un Chant d'amour*, he points out that:

Jean Genet has created the class of film that only a
true poet would conceive of. The great poet Jean
Genet has given himself the unprecedented luxury of
making a film that will never be one of the exclusive
shows at the cinemas of the Champs-Elysées, a film
whose poetic nature excludes it from being publicly
shown in club cinemas or film festivals the world
over. He has created a film for himself.[8]

Henri Langlois gave *Un Chant d'amour* its public premiere at the Cinémathèque Française in 1954, screening a version cut of its sexually explicit material. But as Nico Papatakis points out, even if the film did not contain erotic scenes, it was in every way a gay love story, and therefore scandalous and subject to censorship. *Un Chant d'amour* was generally unavailable for public viewing in France for the following twenty years. In 1964 Nico Papatakis described the climate of censorship in France to Jonas Mekas:

> *Q: Do you think this film could be shown in France today?*
> *A: No. No. Regarding censorship, France is one of the most reactionary countries in the world. There are myths about France, about the freedom of the spirit, the French spirit, etc. – this is mythical. The French government today is the most reactionary government in the history of France.*[9]

Exhibition Histories

United States of America

In 1964 Papatakis sold prints of *Un Chant d'amour* to the avant-garde Film Makers' Co-Operative in New York. Papatakis had gone to the States to co-produce John Cassavetes' film *Shadows* in 1959, and *The Connection* directed by Shirley Clarke in 1960. He was a film director in his own right by 1962 with *Les Abysses*. He had also taken the chanteuse Nico (she took this name from him) from Paris to New York where he introduced her to Andy Warhol.

The Sixties was a time of great achievement in experimental film-making and exhibition in the States. This consequently led to the prosecution and censorship for obscenity of key films such as Jack Smith's *Flaming Creatures* and Kenneth Anger's *Scorpio Rising*. The uncertificated screening of *Un Chant d'amour* in New York in March

1964 was raided by the police who brutalised the organiser, Jonas Mekas (who was the leader of the Film Makers Co-Operative), imprisoning him and informing him that he deserved to be shot in front of the cinema screen for 'dirtying America'. Mekas' 'Report From Jail' was printed in his 'Movie Journal' column in the *Village Voice*:

> *The detectives who seized the Genet film,* Un Chant d'amour, *did not know who Genet was. When I told them that Genet was an internationally known artist, I was told it was my fantasy...*[10]

The New York case against *Un Chant d'amour* was eventually dismissed by the District Attorney, but not before it had drained its defendants of thousands of dollars which could have been used for creative work. A print of the film was later acquired by the Museum of Modern Art in New York.

Later the same year, a hotel room screening of *Un Chant d'amour* organised by Saul Landau for the San Francisco Mime Troupe was also raided, and the print seized by the police. Landau brought suit to show the film without police interference, but after viewing it – twice – the Alameda County Superior Court concluded that it was obscene. On appeal, the District Court of Appeal of California affirmed this judgment, concluding that the film was 'hard-core pornography' and therefore banned in Berkeley. The Court stated that *Un Chant d'amour*

> ... *goes far beyond customary limits of candor in offensively depicting certain unorthodox sexual practices and relationships ... Because of the nature of the medium, we think a motion picture of sexual scenes may transcend the bounds of the constitutional*

guarantee long before a frank description of the same
scenes in the written word. We cannot here disregard
the potent visual impact of the movie in [various
sexual acts] without any clear reference or relation to
a dominant theme.[11]

In the Court's opinion Genet's literary renown did not exempt the film from restrictions of exhibition, and the words of one of Landau's own witnesses were used against the defence when the film was cited as a transitional work in Genet's development from a novelist to a dramatist, barely recognisable as part of his oeuvre. The Court declined to find 'any matter of social importance (including artistic merit)' in *Un Chant d'amour*, nor any discernible plot, story line, dominant theme or character development. The film was characterised as a failure:

The erotic scenes recur with increasing intensity and
without direction toward any well-defined, whole-
some idea, through scene after scene. The various
sexual acts are graphically pictured or emphatically
suggested with nothing omitted except those sexual
consummations which are plainly suggested but
meaningfully omitted and thus by the very fact of
omission emphasised. If the film was intended as an
artistic portrayal, it clearly failed in its endeavor.[12]

In 1968 a *Life* magazine article on Genet included a quotation of his dandy response to the Courts of California in finding *Un Chant d'amour* obscene:

I believe I saw something like that in the papers. But
really, if these gentlemen had something to say to me,
they should have communicated with me directly.

That is the way things are done among men of the world.[13]

France

By the late 1960s *Un Chant d'amour* was being shown occasionally on the 'underground' or experimental film-making circuit in Paris. Screenings increased notably from the end of 1974 when the enthusiastic Collectif Jeune Cinéma bought a bootleg print from West Germany to distribute in Paris. By this time, as Papatakis points out, there had been a certain relaxation of film censorship, and so, as he had never recouped the film's costs, he collaborated with film producer Anatole Dauman and his assistant Monique Lange to submit it to the Centre Nationale de la Cinématographie for a censor's visa and the annual producer's award for the best 'new' film of 1975.

Although it had obviously been made twenty-five years previously, *Un Chant d'amour* was awarded the equivalent of nine million old French francs. When informed of his film's success, Genet was furious and took immediate action to prohibit its imminent public exhibition. He wrote an open letter to Michel Guy, then Minister of Culture, which was published in *L'Humanité* on 13 August 1975:

> *Your offices have been irresponsible, they have sent me a letter of congratulations for a prize which has been awarded to me because of my film* Un Chant d'amour *directed some time ago.*
> *Here's the truth: the film in question, I wrote the scenario, I filmed it, I did the editing and re-editing, that was more than twenty years ago. But in order to obtain the prize of around nine million old francs, some producer has presented it to a number of commissioning bodies – including the censorship body –*

*as being a film from last year. It's perhaps important
that you know the names of the people in your offices
or its annexes, taking from it half of nine million.*

*I'm writing to you especially to tell you that I refuse
all prize or subsidy awarded by your commissions.
You should congratulate yourself, sir, because you
have made me virtuous. If I don't denounce this
prize, it would deauthenticate the sense of my work
(you cannot give a money prize to a film made a long
time ago as if it was the most recent fulfilment of my
activity).*

*So, since the law recognises me as owner of my artistic
creation it gives me the right to modify or even reject
work that I judge to be of defect, the chance is finally
given to me to respect the law.*

*And so again, people less charitable than me could
think themselves able to see, behind the attribution
of this prize, a really shadey political operation with
the goal of trapping a writer who continues to doubt
the liberalism of your government, and who refuses
censorship and praise coming from it.*

*I add also that I will always oppose the public projec-
tion of the film, which I made in order to sell copies
to particular people, since in parallel I also sold the
limited editions of my books, I reserve myself the
right (it's the law!) to modify the definitive form. I
want nobody – apart from myself – to be able to
judge this 'sketch of a sketch'!*[14]

Genet reasserted his position on the film in an interview published a few months later in the French edition of *Playboy*, stating his
refusal to grant any producer the right to market *Un Chant d'amour*.

Genet's denunciation of the prize and his ironic threat to take Papatakis to court resulted in an unresolved rift between the two, a fate that befell many of Genet's close friends, including Paule Thévenin. Genet had succeeded in delimiting the public availability of *Un Chant d'amour* in Paris, which was compounded by the decline in operations of the Collectif Jeune Cinéma through financial pressures, and by the destruction of Genet's print (entrusted to the Cinémathèque Française by Madame Thévenin on 5 December 1975) in 1980.

Great Britain

In 1971 Papatakis sold a few 16mm prints of *Un Chant d'amour* to independent distributors in London. The young composer Gavin Bryars was commissioned by Memorial Enterprises, the company belonging to Michael Medwin and Albert Finney (at this time Finney was the husband of Papatakis' ex-wife, Anouk Aimée) to add a musical soundtrack to their print only. Bryars was already known for his work composing experimental film soundtracks for the cineaste Stephen Dwoskin. Bryars created a multichannelled soundtrack which gloriously mixes timpani beat, animal noises and birdsong to a seductive effect in conjunction with Genet's images. He worked from the viewer on the edit suite, and has never seen *Un Chant d'amour* projected either with or without his soundtrack. This print belonged to The Other Cinema Film Distributors (later Metro Pictures) and remained the only copy ever to have been given a permanent soundtrack. It was withdrawn from distribution in 1990. In a 1964 interview Jonas Mekas asks (an anonymous) Papatakis about Genet's creative decisions:

> Q: *There was never talk about adding a soundtrack?*
> A: *No, never. Music, perhaps. But – no.*[15]

Un Chant d'amour was premiered in London in February 1971 at the New Cinema Club in Wardour Street as part of a programme of short films entitled 'Acts of Love', including Dwoskin's *Moment 1*, Takhito Iimura's *A1 (Love)* and Carolee Schneeman's *Fuses*. Papatakis attended the first screening of *Un Chant d'amour* in London and later recalled how disappointed he had been seeing the film again for the first time in twenty years. In Papatakis' mind the film, once great, had been diminished by time, and he cites Genet's same disillusionment, coming from his increased political activism (Genet aligned himself to racial causes – the Black Panthers and the PLO – and never to gay liberation), as being the impetus behind his refusal of the award and the film's intended release in 1975:

> *In the beginning [Genet] recognised his film as a good one. But he evolved politically. He thought that socially speaking it was not a good film. Politically, aesthetically, he was not pleased anymore with the film. You can understand that if you really see the film coldly, without thinking it's by Jean Genet. It's a very romantic film, a very sentimental film. It's a very SOFT film – a 'fleur bleue', a little romance. It's a love story between two prisoners. One of them dreams that he has this bucolic thing. My opinion is that his film was very daring in the beginning when he made it, but things have evolved. In censorship homosexuality is not banned as it was before – it's recognised now. What little remains of the film is the story between two characters, the dream of one who is very much in love with the other and things like that. So you can understand that he wouldn't really like it by the end of his life.*[16]

Un Chant d'amour was shown regularly and without issue or censorship on the experimental, art and repertory circuits in the

United Kingdom. However, in early 1989 Hull Town Council refused its Film Theatre permission for a screening of the uncertificated print. The councillors' chairman felt that it would be equally offensive to both homosexuals and heterosexuals, and stated:

> *If any ordinary member of the public came to see it I think they would be shocked and offended. The Film Theatre leaflet says it is poetic, but I didn't see anything poetic about it.*

Soon after the banning of the film in Hull, the British Film Institute took receipt of two brand new prints, one of which is the first ever to be struck in 35mm, negotiated from Nico Papatakis in response to the increasingly dilapidated condition of the prints which had been in distribution and in demand since 1971.

Notes

1. Jacques Natteau (born Etienne Chinminatto in Constantinople, 1920) worked as a cameraman from 1938 and was cinematographer on the following films:
   1938: *La Bête humaine* (Jean Renoir)
   1950: *L'Aiguille rouge* (Emil Edwin Reinert)
   1952: *La Neige était sale* (Luis Saslavsky)
   1953: *Le Blé en herbe* (Claude Autant-Lara)
         Le Bon dieu sans confessions (Claude Autant-Lara)
   1954: *Le Rouge et le noir* (Claude Autant-Lara)
         Tam-Tam (Gian Gaspare Napolitano)
   1955: *Marguerite de la nuit* (Claude Autant-Lara)
   1956: *Celui qui doit mourir* (Jules Dassin)
         La Traversée de Paris (Claude Autant-Lara)
   1957: *Les Misérables* (Jean-Paul Le Chanois)
   1958: *Un Drôle de dimanche* (Marc Allegret)
         En Cas de malheur (Claude Autant-Lara)
   1959: *Le Joueur* (Claude Autant-Lara)
         La Jument verte (Claude Autant-Lara)
         Normandie-Niemen (Jean Dreville)
   1960: *Le Bois des amants* (Claude Autant-Lara)
         Tu ne tueras point (Claude Autant-Lara)
         Vive Henri IV, vive l'amour (Claude Autant-Lara)

1961: *Le Comte de Monte Cristo* (Claude Autant-Lara)
Phaedra (Jules Dassin)
1962: *Du Mouron pour les petits oiseaux* (Marcel Carné)
Le Meurtrier (Claude Autant-Lara)
1963: *Le Magot de Josefa* (Claude Autant-Lara)

2. Interview with Ginette and Lucien Sénemaud, Le Cannet, 13 September 1988 by the author and Edmund White. Ginette answered most of the questions, as Lucien is reluctant to talk about the past for two reasons: in loyalty to Genet who was against interviews; because he does not wish to discuss his criminal past and gay relationship with Genet.

3. There is a discrepancy between the initials B.A.A.D.C. shown on the film and the phrase 'Bonjour aux amis de malheur' as given in *Journal du Voleur*. An alternative word for 'malheur' that begins with the letter C might be 'contretemps' or 'calamité'.

4. André Fraigneau, *Cocteau on Film* (London: Dennis Dobson Ltd, 1954).

5. Interview with Edmund White, Paris, 1987.

6. '1989: Flames In The Night' (Kenneth Anger interviewed by Rebekah Wood), *Into the Pleasure Dome – the films of Kenneth Anger*, eds. Jayne Pilling and Mike O'Pray (London: BFI Distribution, 1989).

7. *The Paris and New York Diaries of Ned Rorem 1951–1961* (San Francisco: North Point Press, 1983), p. 118.

8. Translated by Stuart Burleigh, 1990.

9. Jonas Mekas, 'On Genet and *Un Chant d'amour*', *Movie Journal* (New York: Collier Books), p. 165.

10. 'Report from Jail', ibid., p. 129.

11. Edward de Grazia and Roger K. Newman, *Banned Films: Movies, Censors & The First Amendment* (New York/London: R. K. Bowker Company, 1982), p. 288.

12. Ibid.

13. Robert Wernick, 'The Three Kings of Bedlam', *Life* magazine, vol. 64, pt. 5, 1968, p. 69.

14. Translated by Stephen Barber, 1988.

15. *Movie Journal*, p. 165.
When shown in cinemas, the film is usually projected silent, or with the projectionist's choice of an instrumental musical accompaniment. One advantage of having music played over the film is that it helps to block out distracting sounds in the cinema.

16. Interview with the author, Paris, 1987 (see Appendix I).

Title shot: 'Un Chant d'amour PAR JEAN GENET' written in white letters on a stone wall that is also graffitied with an arrow-pierced heart, and flowers.

A stone wall meets a stone path bordered by a grass verge. A man in a prison warder's uniform appears, looking up and out of the frame as he walks. He stops centrally. The shot cuts to a close-up of him gazing.

Two adjacent barred cell windows, an arm emerging from each. The left hand repeatedly swings a bouquet of blossom attached to a string, but each time the right hand fails to grasp the flowers.

The warder stares, then walks out of the frame. Fade to black.

Fade up from black onto the bare feet of a man standing on a roughly tiled cell floor. The camera pans up his body, which shifts and sways slightly in a gentle dance. This is the younger convict, dressed in white trousers, his thumbs stuck in the pockets, and a white vest which reveals an androgynous face above a compass tattoo on his upper arm. He gazes into the distance as he turns in a circular dance.

An older, darker prisoner wearing a thick jumper and rough dark trousers paces up and down in his cell. He knocks on the wall, listens, and then strikes fist into palm in frustration. The prisoner knocks again.

The younger convict stands still, smiling slightly. He flicks back his short hair with his hand, then runs it over his tattoo.

The older prisoner is pressed up against the cell wall, kissing it gently. His eyes are full of tears.

The younger convict dances circularly, one hand caressing his tattoo, the other cupping his genitals.

In profiled silhouette the older prisoner inserts a straw into a tiny hole in his cell wall.

The younger convict stops still and stares at the straw emerging through his cell wall, on which there is graffitied an enormous penis.

The straw is seen in close-up, coming through the cell wall. Smoke discharges from its tip.

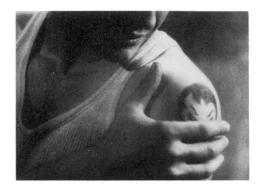

The younger convict turns away from the cell wall and looks down at his tattoo. Smiling, in close-up, he caresses the face on his upper arm, and recommences his dance.

The older prisoner withdraws the straw from the wall, and exhales massively. He stubs the butt of his cigarette out on a knot in a wooden table, and puts some gum in his mouth. He chews it up then sticks the pulp into the hole in the wall, sealing it with his wet and dirty fingers. The prisoner drops down onto his bunk, and caresses his thickly haired chest at the opening of his jumper. He rubs his genitals, returns to his chest, hands working in circular movements. His mouth forms a silent groan as he reaches into his pocket to clasp his cock. The older prisoner rushes to embrace the cell wall, and there is a close-up of his erect penis flicking up against the rough stone. He turns a full circle against the wall.

The younger convict continues to dance, holding his tattoo.

The warder turns the corner of a dark corridor lined with cell doors. Smoking a cigarette, he approaches a door and pushing back the spy-hole cover, peeps in.

A man in a dark suit stands in his cell, back to the camera, pictured from his waist to his knees. He is masturbating, and turns slightly, his erection half visible to the camera.

The warder moves to another cell door, marked 'Meurtre' (murder). He peeps in through the spy hole.

A young prisoner lies on his bunk, topless, his legs up the cell wall as he masturbates, a cloth covering his groin.

The warder is peeping through the spyhole. He moves to the next door cell and opens its hatch to look in.

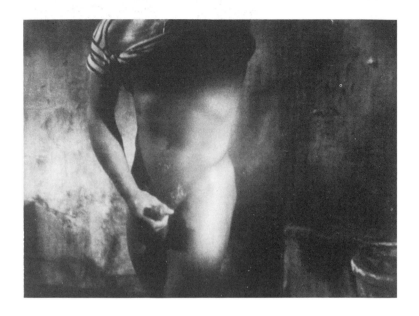

Inside the cell a nude man is washing, he soaps his shiny skin as he stands in front of a basin, framed from chest to knees, back to the camera. The prisoner turns around, and is seen to be soaping his erection; he walks across the cell and the camera pans upwards with him, revealing that he wears a crucifix around his neck and striped t-shirt rolled up across his shoulders and that he is grinning broadly as he simultaneously soaps his hair and rubs his oiled erection.

The warder's face is framed by the rectangular hatch. He is smiling, and shifting slightly.

Grinning at the camera, the prisoner continues to soap, rub, masturbate.

The warder shuts the hatch of the cell door and flicks ash from his cigarette. He adjusts his crotch, then moves towards another cell door.

A young lithe black prisoner performs an undulating dance in his cell. He is bare chested, the flies of his white trousers are open, and he holds exposed his long, flaccid penis.

Craning to see, the warder's face is framed by the rectangular hatch.

The black prisoner's dance becomes faster, arms outstretched he spins in a circle, penis dangling. The dance slows down as the prisoner starts to masturbate, then he sinks face down upon his bunk, writhing.

The warder walks to another cell door, he touches the spy-hole cover then rejects it and moves to the neighbouring door which is labelled 'Meurtre'. He looks around him and spits out his cigarette butt before peeping in.

The warder's eye is seen in extreme close-up from inside the cell, framed by the circular spyhole, as the cover is drawn back from the outside.

The younger convict sits on his bunk picking at the hole in the toe of his woollen sock.

The warder peers in at him.

The convict picks a crumb from his filthy toe and examines it in detail before peeling the thick sock off his richly haired leg. Dirt and texture are emphasised.

The warder's eye peers through the spyhole.

The younger convict cushions his head from the cell wall with one hand, and cradles his crotch with the other.

The warder's eye peers through the spyhole.

The younger convict's armpit is seen in extreme close-up, muscle pulsing under skin and hair.

His throat is seen in close detail, he swallows.

The younger convict's leg is bent at the knee as he reclines, forming a triangular frame through which one can see his hand fondling his groin.

He lightly licks his lips, and opens his eyes.

The warder stands at the spyhole, beneath the sign 'Meurtre'.

The younger convict sits on his bunk, one arm raised still to cushion his head from the cell wall, one hand resting between his legs. He moves this hand slowly up his chest and starts to kiss it gently, up to the arm then back down to the hand. Arms crossed over his chest, the kisses are transferred to the other arm and hand. The younger convict sits up and taking his bent knee in both hands, kisses it also. He looks at the cell wall and knocks on it twice.

The warder moves to the neighbouring cell and puts his eye to the spyhole.

The older prisoner repeatedly kisses the cell wall, around the navel-like plugged hole. His eyes are shut.

The younger convict knocks on the cell wall with his fist. He stops to listen, then knocks again.

The older prisoner continues to kiss the cell wall.

The younger convict pulls straws from his mattress, tossing them away until he finds a large one. He inserts the straw into the hole in the cell wall.

Smiling, the older prisoner rolls a cigarette.

The younger convict waits, lips parted, in front of the straw.

The older prisoner draws on the cigarette, then exhales into the straw.

Smoke is discharged from the end of the straw, the younger convict closes his mouth around its tip and inhales greedily. Smoke spills out of his mouth and nostrils.

The older prisoner exhales into the straw, withdraws to drag on the cigarette butt, then exhales again.

The younger convict gulps at the smoking straw.

The older prisoner exhales into the straw.

Sucking in the smoke, the younger convict pulls the straw slowly out of the hole in the cell wall.

As the straw vanishes into the wall the older prisoner's mouth follows it, still exhaling.

The straw is drawn from the hole, smoke drifting from its tip.

The older prisoner continues to exhale, smoke spilling over the stone. He turns away from the cell wall and clutches his crotch, then stubs the cigarette butt out in the knot on the surface of a wooden table.

Close up of the younger convict's face as he lies back and smokes. He exhales and opens his eyes.

The older prisoner sits hunched on his bunk, biting his hand. He jumps up and moves towards the cell door.

The warder quickly shuts the spyhole cover of the older prisoner's cell door and, rubbing his crotch, moves back to the younger convict's door. He lifts the spyhole cover.

Close up of the younger convict's face as he reclines, stroking his throat and flaring his nostrils.

The warder's eye looks in, framed by the round spyhole.

Extreme close up of the younger convict's face gazing distantly.

The older prisoner knocks on the cell wall.

The younger convict arises suddenly, stares briefly at the cell wall, then moves away. He walks towards some clothing hanging on the back wall but stops, and looking back over his shoulder shouts, looking aggravated. The younger convict turns, holding his crotch and then freezes. He looks slowly at the cell door.

The warder's eye looks in, framed by the round spyhole. [This shot was edited in upside down.]

The younger convict is seen from waist to thigh, his belt sticking out and hand moving in his pocket.

The warder's eye looks in, framed by the spyhole.

The younger convict looks towards the cell door, smiling ironically.

The warder moves away from the younger convict's cell door. He closes his eyes, and the shot fades to black.

Fade up from black. Against a black background white blossom swings five times from the left to the right; each time a hand fails to catch it.

Against a black background the luminous white bodies of two nude men embrace, a flower held in the mouth of one of them, the other is the warder. They kiss, and the warder encloses the flower in his mouth. The flower reappears, mangled by their kisses, as the two men part.

The torsos of two men, one wearing a shirt and the other bare chested. The latter writhes as the former thrusts his hand down inside the back of his trousers.

Back from his fantasy, the warder stands outside the cell door, looking disturbed. He unbuttons his uniform jacket to withdraw a gun from inside, and moves towards the neighbouring cell door. The warder unlocks it and enters.

Inside the cell the warder closes the door behind him. Transferring the gun to his left hand, the warder unbuttons the bottom of his jacket and unbuckles his belt.

The older prisoner stands staring.

The warder approaches.

The older prisoner moves backwards, his eyes fixed down.

The warder approaches, raises his belt then thrashes it forwards.

The older prisoner raises his arms in self-protection.

Grimacing with the effort, the warder thrashes his belt down repeatedly. His twisted face is shown in close-up.

Close-up of the older prisoner's panic-stricken face, his arms remaining raised in self protection.

A sweat breaks out on the warder's forehead with the exertion of the continued thrashing.

The older prisoner mouths a word or groan.

The warder's mouth stretches into a grin as he thrashes.

Looking back over his shoulder with a frozen half smile the younger convict takes his jacket from a peg on the cell wall, puts it on and moves forwards.

Shaken, the older prisoner stands laughing in his cell, then sinks to his knees. Fade to black.

Fade up from black. The older prisoner and the younger convict are walking forwards across a hillside covered with trees. Pushing thin branches out of their way, the older prisoner talks animatedly to the younger convict who has his thumbs stuck in his pockets and a branch of white blossom held in front of his flies. The two men are dressed in the same clothes worn in the jail sequences previously.

They stop either side of a thick tree trunk. Leaning against it, the younger convict looks up.

The bare branches of the tree, as seen from below.

The older prisoner smiles slightly, but stops as he glances down, strong shadows cast across his face.

Close-up of the younger convict's hand holding the branch of blossom in front of his flies, his thumb caressing the petals.

The older prisoner looks back up, smiling again.

The younger convict lies down on the grass, and the older prisoner joins him, resting his head on the other's belly, placing his arm across the other's leg. The older prisoner looks up into the younger convict's face smiling, and the other raises his head to look back, but immediately jumps up and chases behind the tree, peeping out from behind it.

The older prisoner gets up, smiling, and hugs the tree trunk. He peers around the side, then jumps back as the younger convict suddenly appears.

The older prisoner stands by the tree trunk as the younger convict's hand rests on the bark, then disappears around the side.

The younger convict darts around the back of the tree and down the hillside. He freezes on his haunches and looks back up the hill, grinning.

The older prisoner hugs the tree trunk, smiling sadly.

The younger convict looks back up the hill, waiting, grinning.

The older prisoner gazes back for a moment, then moves away from the tree.

The younger convict waits, still looking back up the hill, then he starts to run, chased by the older prisoner. They disappear into trees and bushes, clutching at the foliage.

The younger convict leads the chase through a wooded area, pursued by the older prisoner.

The two men run into a clearing, and stop to catch their breath. The older prisoner snatches the branch of blossom from the outstretched hand of the younger convict.

Grim faced, the older prisoner inhales the scent of the flowers.

The older prisoner is on his knees in the cell, he collapses, clutching at the bedclothes.

The warder looks down, breathing hard. Fade to black.

Fade up from black. Against a black background white blossom swings three times from the left to the right; each time a hand fails to catch it.

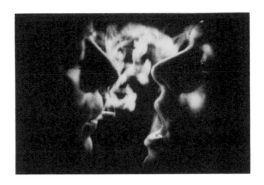

Against a black background two men face each other. The man on the left has a cigarette in his mouth, smoke drifting from its tip; with his lips he turns the lighted end inside his mouth. The two men kiss, enclosing the cigarette between their mouths.

Against a black background the warder holds another man carefully by the neck and chest, rubbing the throat and holding the head back. He slides his hand down the other's body. Both men are naked.

Against a black background, seen from waist to thighs, a man stands in his underpants, a hand beneath the material circles towards his genitals. A second hand shoots downwards and grabs the hidden hand. The two hands clutch and rub together as the body twists slightly.

The warder stands in the cell, looking down, breathing hard.

The older prisoner is collapsed against the bed, then hauls himself upon it. Lying on his back, he raises a knee and clutches his groin.

The warder retreats towards the cell door, still looking down, breathing hard and appearing numbed. Fade to black.

Fade up from black. The older prisoner stands in the wood, inhaling the scent of the blossom.

The younger convict suddenly grabs the flowers and runs into the trees; the older prisoner gives chase.

The two men enter a clearing and stop against some thin trees, the older prisoner falling to his knees in front of the younger convict, supporting himself with a branch.

On his knees the older prisoner fumbles with the branch of blossom. He appears tired, and unable to know what to do with the flowers. Abruptly the younger convict grabs the blossom and stuffs it inside the older prisoner's jersey.

The younger convict looks down grimly.

The older prisoner reaches up and pulls the younger convict across his shoulders, where he lies limply. The older prisoner carries the other away. Fade to black.

Fade up from black. The older prisoner walks through the woods carrying the younger convict. He stops to look around him, and takes a gentle hold of the younger convict's dangling hand. The older prisoner continues walking.

The older prisoner carries the younger through a densely overgrown thicket.

The older prisoner reaches a clearing as he emerges from the trees. He looks around and then finds a spot to lay the younger convict down.

As the younger convict sinks to the ground, the older prisoner leans back and looks down at him.

Close-up of the younger convict's face as he lies on the ground; strong shadows of branches are cast across his forehead, he puckers his lips slightly and flares his nostrils.

An extreme close-up of the older prisoner's torso, breathing hard. The blossom is held in the place of his heart, and is revealed in the opening between the rough wool and his chest.

Close-up of the younger convict's face, eyes closed.

The older prisoner looks down, his face darkened by stubble and deep lines.

Extreme close-up of a throat swallowing.

The older prisoner is seen from behind, kneeling on the ground, his muddy boot soles foregrounded. The younger convict's boots stick out from beneath the older prisoner, who then moves to one side.

The older prisoner lies down beside the prone body, and rolls up the younger convict's vest as he blinks in the bright sunlight. The older prisoner unbuckles the younger convict's belt. He strokes the older prisoner's hair.

The warder retreats towards the cell door, which opens behind him, still pointing the gun.

The warder stands calmly in the jail corridor in front of a cell door marked with three letters.

The older prisoner lies on his cell bed rubbing his groin. He suddenly flings himself face downwards, and writhes.

The warder stands in the jail corridor, an expression of composure on his face. Fade to black.

Against a black background white blossom swings twice from left to right; each time a hand fails to catch it.

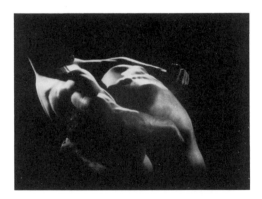

Against a black background two nude men, muscular and shining, 'wrestle' or embrace. One holds the other in a gentle headlock, as they slowly turn.

Against a black background a nude man rests his head against the naked thigh of another, who strokes his hair. Although hidden, their actions suggest fellatio.

Against a black background an upside down nude man hugs the upright naked torso of another in a '69' position.

Against a black background two nude men clamber over one another as they each crawl face downwards in opposite directions.

Against a black background the exerted face of a dark-haired man is caught between the naked thighs of another.

Against a black background a nude man holds his face to another's abdomen and kneads his oiled buttocks, suggesting fellatio.

Against a black background a nude man crawls on his belly while another wriggles face upwards, covering his genitals with his hand, in the opposite direction.

Against a black background a nude man lies face down, seen from shoulders to buttocks, writhing. Another plunges downwards, across his waist, and straightens suggesting penetration.

The warder stands in front of a cell door marked 'Meurtre'.

The older prisoner lies on the ground in the forest clearing, unbuttoning the younger convict's trousers.

Close-up of the warder's uniformed chest as he reaches inside his jacket to withdraw his gun, which he points forwards. The warder wears a tie with the motif of a bicycle.

Close-up of the older prisoner's face, his eyes closed. He looks up as the gun slides across his cheek and into his mouth.

Arm outstretched, the warder holds his head back, eyes closed and nostrils flaring in ecstasy.

The jail corridor is empty. Fade to black.

Fade up from black. The warder walks up the stone path by the wall outside the jail. He stops to turn and look back, hand in pocket, his jacket unbuttoned and open.

Two adjacent barred cell windows, an arm emerging from

each. The left hand twice swings a bouquet of blossom attached to a string, but each time the right hand fails to grasp the flowers.

The older prisoner stands by his cell wall, knocking on it and listening repeatedly. He strikes fist into palm in frustration, walking away from the wall and then back again, to knock and listen, repeatedly. Fade to black.

Fade up from black. The warder is looking back, but then turns and walks away.

An arm emerges from each of the two adjacent barred cell windows. The left hand swings a bouquet of blossom attached to a string, which is suddenly caught by the right hand, and pulled inside the cell. Both hands are slowly withdrawn into their respective barred windows. Fade to black.

Fade up from black. Graffitied centrally on the stone of a cell wall are the dates AVRIL–JUIN 1950. In the bottom left corner of the frame are the initials M.A.V. Centre bottom right are the initials B.A.A.D.C. Centre top there are ten digits scored off.

Notes

1. In 1964 Jonas Mekas asked Nico Papatakis whether there was a film script for *Un Chant d'amour* or if Genet had worked from notes. He replied:

   > *No, not that I'm aware of. He kept a sort of mental script. He knew in advance what he wanted to do. I don't think he wrote anything. He was shooting every day and night.*

   Movie Journal (NY: Collier Books, 1972), p. 164.

   However, Ginette Sénemaud asserts that Genet was always scribbling, and it seems unlikely that he would have created *Un Chant d'amour* without the use of notes and/or writings. The film has a tight, logical structure which defies the notion of free improvisation and random imagery. Yet certainly no formal script, nor any notes, are known to exist.

   This descriptive shot-by-shot breakdown is taken from the definitive twenty-five minute version of the film supervised by Genet in 1950.

Notes On Themes and Images

With the benefit of hindsight, surveying sixty years of international cinema culture, *Un Chant d'amour* may be categorised as one of the 'film poems', a lyrical avant-garde work comparable to the films of Jean Cocteau, Kenneth Anger, Maya Deren and Nagisa Oshima. But abandoning this privileged perspective it is difficult to find *Un Chant d'amour* a genuine precedent. Nico Papatakis has denied any cinematic influences upon the film, and so in order to both explicate and locate it as a part of Genet's oeuvre, it is more useful to see connections with his novels and plays prior to 1950. In the context of a chronology, *Un Chant d'amour* comes at the approximate boundary between his written and his staged work. This fact was used against the film in the US obscenity trial of 1964, as it was then cited as a transitional work, unrepresentative of Genet's oeuvre. However, he displayed an interest in the cinematic visualisation of ideas as early as the forties. Furthermore, throughout Genet's life's work he demonstrated an ongoing use of the same images, structures and thematic concerns, whether his medium was that of literature, theatre, radio or film.

Narrative Structure

Genet's narrative structure is characteristically complex, with stories being told through a fragmentation of time and space. In *Notre Dame des fleurs* the tale of Divine, Darling, Our Lady and co. is fabricated by the narrator (Genet) as he lies on his cell bunk. The novel intercuts between the two worlds, both of which are created by the writer, but with one being represented as 'reality' and the other as 'fantasy'. In the play *Haute Surveillance* the story is divided up by the different specified levels of the prison. This was theatrically developed in *Le Balcon*, *Les Nègres* and *Les Paravents*, as action takes place on different levels of the stage.

In *Un Chant d'amour* the narrative is divided into three stylistically separate sections: the prison, the warder's fantasy and the older prisoner's daydream. The prison is signified by interior cell sets; the warder's fantasy by an abstraction of swinging white blossom, and white bodies in sexual tableaux, chiaroscuro-lit against a dense black background; and the prisoner's daydream characteristically takes place in a forest exterior. These three strands are tightly intercut and on first viewing the film can cause a confusion of time, space and character, although the distinctions are in fact methodically and conventionally made and the editing follows a precise paradigm of 'prison/warder's fantasy/prison/older prisoner's daydream/prison', etc. which repeats itself three times.

Within a complex narrative structure Genet's work is often autobiographical (be this of his life or his fantasies), repeatedly using the setting of a prison, and wrought with recurring themes and motifs, such as those of masturbation; dance; the gun in the mouth; power relationships; the cell wall; racial difference; flowers. In *Un Chant d'amour* Genet renders their cinematic visualisation for the only time in his career, and these images can be compared to their literary equivalents in his novels.

The Cell Wall

The prison sequences in *Un Chant d'amour* constitute the film's given 'reality' (as opposed to what is signified as a character's subjective fantasy or daydream). The imposing cell wall of *Un Chant d'amour* becomes the focus for the older prisoner's sexual activity, as he kisses it tenderly and flicks his penis against the rough stone. This eroticisation of the wall is anticipated in *Notre dame des fleurs*:

> *He puts his cheek to the wall. With a kiss he licks the vertical surface, and the greedy plaster sucks in his saliva. Then a shower of kisses.[1]*

This passage can be compared to the scene in which the older prisoner kisses his cell wall around its navel-like plugged up smoking hole in *Un Chant d'amour*. The smoking sequence is one of the most erotic in the film, as the wall is penetrated by a straw which carries its discharge of smoke from the mouth of the older prisoner to that of the younger convict.

The cell wall is graffitied with images of penises, flowers and initials. The film's closing credits feature the letters M.A.V. and B.A.A.D.C., also described in *Miracle de la rose*:

> *It was amidst hearts and flowers that the inscription M.A.V. suddenly brought me back to my cell at Petite Roquette.[2]*

In the same novel Genet recalls having seen the words 'tattooed Jean' engraved into a cell wall, but due to a deformation of the crude lettering he reads it as 'tortured Jean'. He also explains the meaning of different tattoos: for example, a wild rose on the thigh indicates 'the jerk' (the one who gets passively fucked). In *Un Chant d'amour* the younger convict strokes the androgyne-faced tattoo on his upper arm.

The graffiti on the cell wall is, like tattooed skin, a sublimation of sexual energy and the eroticisation of a boundary. In the film the cell wall crucially functions as the boundary that keeps its prisoner apart from (sexual interaction with) his neighbour, object of his desire. This physical deprivation and separation makes possible the flight of the prisoner's masturbatory fantasies, as it made necessary Genet's writing in jail.

The confines of the cell wall turn the prisoner back in upon himself, which Genet characterises in terms of circularity. In *Miracle de la rose* he describes the exercise period at Fontevrault prison as one in which the convicts march monotonously around a shit-bucket, placed centrally for their public (in)convenience. The punishment at Mettray Borstal for boys caught masturbating was to walk twenty kilometres in a circle every day for eight days. In *Haute Surveillance* Green Eyes chants 'circling round, circling round, circling round', while attempting to dance backwards through time.

This circularity is evident in *Un Chant d'amour*, thematically in the prisoners' movements in both dance and masturbation and formally as the closing sequence of the film recalls its opening shots both suggesting the repetitiousness of the prison narrative and recalling the film loop of early pornography. By turning the prisoner in on himself, the cell wall maintains desire, which would otherwise be inhibited or lost at orgasm. So it is a boundary that is both hated – punched, marked and penetrated – and adored – caressed and kissed. The eroticisation of separation is carried over into the older prisoner's daydream, in his game of chase with his lover, by the younger convict's swoon and by the boundaries of the two men's clothing. The antithesis of this is the action of the warder – free to move between the boundaries of the jail, to look inside and to enter the cell, brutalising its prisoner – and of his fantasy, featuring the penetration of clothing and finally of a body.

Flowers

In *Journal du voleur* Genet muses on how his name is that of a flower, the yellow blossomed broom, a prickly shrub which grows isolated in marshland, and with which he feels an affinity:

> *I feel a deep sense of kinship with them ... they know that I am their living, moving, agile representative.*[3]

This identification is part of Genet's comparison between flowers and convicts, and his erotic desire to transpose the two:

> *There is a close relationship between flowers and convicts. The fragility and delicacy of the former are of the same nature as the brutal insensitivity of the latter. My sexual excitement is the oscillation from one to the other. Should I have to portray a convict – or a criminal – I shall so bedeck him with flowers that, as he disappears beneath them, he will himself become a flower, a gigantic and new one.*[4]

There are numerous examples of the equivalence of man to flower in Genet's works, including: 'Notre Dame had the moral and physical character of a flower' (*Notre dame des fleurs*); the idea that to photograph a band of half-stripped young pirate sailors would register as simply a rose upon the photographic plate, and that the autopsy of a condemned murderer would reveal a gigantic rose in place of his heart, while his shackles are transformed into a bouquet (*Miracle de la rose*); '... that was the real Querelle, coming into flower, blossoming, showing the underside of his delicate petals.' (*Querelle de Brest*); 'The big, inflexible, strict pimps, their members in full bloom – I no longer know whether they are lilies or whether lilies and members are not totally they.' (*Notre Dame des fleurs*).

Genet actually achieves the transposition of a man into a flower through the warder's fantasy in *Un Chant d'amour*. In each of its three instances the fantasy is signalled by the image of luminous white blossom swinging towards an outstretched hand, an abstraction of the sight which catches the warder's eye outside the prison at the beginning of the film and thus initiates his investigation. Stylistically the whole of the warder's fantasy is characterised by this chiaroscuro lighting, and the white bodies of the men are photographed to resemble the white blossom, making a visual match and therefore an equivalent in the mind of the viewer.

Although in *Pompes Funèbres* Genet denied that flowers symbolise anything, their appearance in his work is inevitably invested with complex meaning, as the image is made up of opposing public and private significance. That is to say that on the one hand the flower is popularly understood as a lyrical symbol of Romantic love (one which both hints at the sexual in terms of appearance, and functions as a prop of seduction). Flowers are the sign of love, and are therefore loved. But Genet also hated flowers.

In his biographical and theoretical study, *Saint Genet, comédien et martyr* (Saint Genet: Actor and Martyr,[5] Jean-Paul Sartre gives an account of how flowers constituted the boundary that marked the separation between Genet's childhood borstal at Mettray from the freedom of the outside world. In *Miracle de la rose*, an escape is described as: 'breaking the barrier of flowers, fighting my way into the realm of the fabulous'.[6] The imprisoning flowers are pictured as having a point of view on Genet, like that of the warder's inhibiting gaze.

Flowers play a privileged role in *Un Chant d'amour*, as they alone appear in each of the film's three narrative strands. At the beginning of the film the flowers function as the enigma which initiates the warder's investigation (and therefore the film itself), and their seizure signifies the end of the film. The abstraction of this image signals the warder's fantasy, and one of his sexual fantasy tableaux pictures blossom ingested in a kiss between two men. The younger convict holds blossom in front of his fly (a metaphor for his unseen genitals) in the older prisoner's daydream. These flowers become the object of snatch and grab during their game of chase, and are finally stuffed into the jersey of the older prisoner, to be seen beating in the place of his heart.

In *Un Chant d'amour* Genet's multi-faceted visualisation of flowers achieves what the film theoretician Christian Metz has identified as a 'poetic metaphor'.[7]

Racial Difference

The image of a flower being eaten, with its erotic connotations, is used in the warder's fantasy, and repeated in Genet's later play, *Les Nègres*:

> *Whilst you were munching flowers in the twilight, I*
> *was bleeding her, without turning a hair.[8]*

What can be seen in the juxtaposition of this image with that of the flower in *Un Chant d'amour* is the development from an ambiguous poetic metaphor to a much more specific and harder political statement. In *Les Nègres* Genet recognises the public and popular meaning of the flower as a part of white cultural domination. The sign of the flower is used to represent white love, white beauty, white language, and flowers are to be ingested, masticated, spat out and gobbled up again in the Blacks' hatred and annihilation of whiteness. In revolt from their assigned place of abjection the Blacks' task is to reinvent language. The sexual threat of monstrous orality consumes the fragile white flower, which is stripped of its Romanticism and returned to a more down-to-earth state of vegetable nutrition. The vicious eroticism is still implied, as the suggestion is of the consumption of white genitalia by the mythical Black mouth. The character of the white Queen articulates this: '... and now, I die – I must confess – choked by my desire for a Big Black Buck. Black nakedness, thou hast conquered me.'

Genet uses race in two instances in *Un Chant d'amour*: in the representation of the African dancer, pinned down in the cell and objectified as an erotic spectacle, and in the character of the older prisoner – the spurned and frustrated lover – who is played by an Arab and with whom the viewer is invited to identify.

Genet described the childhood origins of this identification:

The schoolteacher asked us to write a little assignment. Each student had to describe his house. I described mine and the teacher said mine was the nicest. He read it out loud and everyone made fun of me and said, 'But it's not his house, he's a foundling', and suddenly such a void opened up, such humiliation. All of a sudden I was such a foreigner – oh,

that's not too strong a word for it. Hating France,
that's not enough, you've got to do more than hate it,
you must vomit it up. After that I could only feel at
home among oppressed people of colour or the
oppressed in revolt against whites. Maybe I'm a
black who's white or pink but still black.[9]

From the late sixties on Genet had largely quit France and spent long periods working for the Black Panthers and the PLO. He campaigned and wrote profusely, a stunning example of which is the document of his May Day speech of 1970. Genet shunned intellectual acclaim – as he did white expatriates – throughout this time. Writing of the Black Panthers, Genet explained how he – the orphan – had been adopted for the second time in his life, now as an old, white-haired baby. Returning to the prison in literary terms in 1970, Genet wrote his startling introduction to George Jackson's book of prison letters, *Soledad Brother*:

> *If white guards superintend a hell in which white*
> *men are jailed, then the white prisoners superintend*
> *another hell inside that one – one in which black men*
> *are jailed.*[10]

In retrospect, Nico Papatakis saw *Un Chant d'amour* as inferior to *Les Nègres* in terms of style, reinvention of language and political content, claiming Genet's same dissatisfaction with the film. Yet it is clear that Genet's politically racial concerns were at work in *Un Chant d'amour*, as it is also evident that he never eschewed the simultaneous identification with and eroticisation of Blacks, nor did he abandon lyrical poeticism, which can be seen in his final book, *Un Captif amoureux* (Prisoner of Love).[11] For both writing, and film-making, can be 'a weapon of liberation and a love poem', when used in the right hands.

Notes

1. *Our Lady of the Flowers* (London: Panther, 1966), p. 101.

2. *Miracle of the Rose* (London: Anthony Blond, 1965), p. 51. (However, the tattoo in *Un Chant d'amour* was a fake. Lucien Sénemaud was, and remained, tattoo-less.)

3. *The Thief's Journal* (London: Penguin, 1985), p. 34.

4. Ibid, p. 5.

5. Jean-Paul Sartre, *Saint Genet: Actor and Martyr* (London: Pantheon, 1983).

6. *Miracle of the Rose*, p. 115.

7. '... the poetic metaphor [is] another kind of précis and a Lacanian example of condensation, a single word with multiple resonances, the meeting-point of several distinct "chains of thought" and hence the point at which overdetermination surfaces.' Christian Metz, *Psychoanalysis and Cinema* (London: Macmillan, 1982), p. 237.

8. *The Blacks* (London: Faber, 1979), p. 39.

9. Quoted in Edmund White, 'Fair is Foul and Foul is Fair', *Literary Review*, September 1986, pp. 59–62.

10. Jean Genet, Introduction to *Soledad Brother* (London: Jonathan Cape, 1971).

11 *Prisoner of Love* (London: Picador, 1989).

Querelle

The Balcony

Appendices

Appendix I

Transposition and the Contradiction of the Film: Interview with Nico Papatakis

Paris 2 October 1987

Jane Giles: *In 1970 you said that the funding of a film is like the funding of a revolution. How was* Un Chant d'amour *funded?*

Nico Papatakis: At that time I had a nightclub named La Rose Rouge and I was making a lot of money because it was very, very successful. I met Jean Genet here in Saint Germain des Prés. He had just published his first book *Notre dame des Fleurs*. We became close friends. In 1946 I opened this place and he used to come. He told me one day that he wanted to make a film – an erotic film. So I said, I'll give you the money to do it, to make the film. That's how it started. So I gave him the money and the budget in the beginning was on the basis of the film made in 16mm in black and white. But after some days of shooting and after we had screened the material we found out that it wasn't very satisfactory to have it done in 16mm. We started doing it all over again in 35mm. Above the nightclub I had a big space which was initially a brasserie, or something, and I wasn't doing anything with that space and so we built the prison sets and he shot it up there.

JG: *Did you help build the sets? Did you do everything?*

NP: No, I just gave the money. He found a man who did them, a professional. Of course, outside, in the beginning of the film when you see the prison – it was filmed at a former prison. In the beginning the film was about 45 minutes, then he cut it to 40 minutes and now it's a version about 25 minutes.

JG: *Why did Genet cut it?*

NP: Because he wasn't satisfied with the longer version of the film. What we tried to do to get back the money was to sell some prints privately because it was impossible for the film to be screened normally in the theatre. So we made some sales but didn't get back the money [laughs].

JG: *How much did you give Genet to make the film?*

NP: Between the 16mm version and the 35mm version the budget was about the equivalent of $40,000 today.

JG: *Or £20,000.*

You had to hire the equipment, hire everything?

NP: Yes.

JG: *And were the actors paid, or were they friends?*

NP: Of course, they were paid. You know it was a very tricky thing to shoot. They were paid very highly because they knew that it was an erotic film. The problem was to find an actor who would do it. One of the actors was Genet's friend at that time.

JG: *Lucien Sénemaud?*

NP: Lucien.

The other was a Tunisian. He was a barber.

Things were said with Genet's boyfriend, but the other people, knowing that they were in an erotic film, the danger was that after a while they would blackmail to get more money. But we avoided that! [laughs] It was a dangerous thing – the whole thing – to shoot without permission and things like that. It was a ridiculously complicated thing. But we managed to finish and then the film was there. The Cinémathèque – Henri Langlois – wanted to show the film, I think it was one year after we finished shooting it. But he screened a very shortened version. All the really erotic bits were taken out.

JG: *Was this the version that had been cut down by Genet to 25 minutes?*

It must have been about 15 minutes long!

NP: 15 minutes.

But at the time it was a big scandal, because it was a story between two prisoners – it was a homosexual film in every way even if the erotic side had not been shown. It was very scandalous.

JG: *So did the production and filming of* Un Chant d'amour *go smoothly or were there problems?*

NP: No, it went smoothly, the problem was for me to have the money. Outside that it was no problem.

JG: *As producer did you choose the cast and crew or did Genet do that?*

NP: It was Genet, he did everything.

JG: *In your interview with Jonas Mekas you mentioned that Jacques Natteau was the cameraman. How did he come to be involved?*

NP: I used to know Jacques Natteau. He lived here [Saint Germain des Prés].

JG: *Genet supervised the editing, but who was the professional editor?*

NP: I don't remember. Was his name Nicolas Coll–?

The set designer was Nicolas Coll– I don't remember his name.

JG: *Do you remember the names of any of the actors?*

NP: No.

JG: *Well, it WAS forty years ago . . .*

NP: None of them were actors.

JG: *I wondered if any of them were the stage actors from the 1949 production of* Haute Surveillance *directed by Genet?*

NP: No.

JG: *I was told that the stage actor André Reybaz was involved. Is this correct?*

NP: No. You mean in the direction of the actors?

JG: *No, as an actor. André Reybaz.*

NP: Yes, maybe he had ... I don't think he ... [laughs]. I don't know ... How would you speak of that? Maybe he [laughs] I'm not sure but I think maybe that in the scene where the sex goes on the wall – maybe he did that. But only for that part.

JG: *You mean as a stand-in?*

NP: As a stand-in! [laughs] I think so, I'm not sure, but my memory is of that. He is a theatre director. I don't know, I'm not sure of that!

JG: *Did Genet hire the other men in the film from La Rose Rouge?*

NP: No, as a matter of fact he didn't hire them in La Rose Rouge. He used to go up to Montmartre. The big man, the older one, was a barber in Montmartre and at the same time he had some women working for him in the streets, a pimp. So Genet was seeing all these people up there and he chose them. That's why I'm always a little scared that these people will make blackmail, start coming and asking for money and things like that.

JG: *In the biography of Henri Langlois it's claimed that he funded* Un Chant d'amour.

NP: No. This is a lie. The proof that I produced it is that the negative is in my name at the laboratory. He can't make any claim about that.

JG: *In this book it's claimed that* Un Chant d'amour *was commissioned for Langlois' festival at Antibes in September 1950.*

That he commissioned a film from Genet, one from Sartre ...

NP: It's just a farce.

Which film of Jean-Paul Sartre did he say he commissioned?

JG: *It didn't say a title, just that the film was commissioned but not finished.*

The Cinémathèque told me that they don't have a print of Un Chant d'amour.

NP: It's true, they don't. I met them the other day – they had a reception for Mankiewicz; by accident I was there – and they asked me for a print. How could Langlois [laughs] say he commissioned the film and have no print of it!? I have to give them one.

JG: *Jean-Paul Morel told me that at the time of his friendship with Paule Thévenin, Genet gave her his copy of the film, and that Madame Thévenin gave it to the Cinémathèque where it was destroyed in a fire. Is this true?*

NP: Yes, I think so.

JG: *Was* Un Chant d'amour *ever banned in France?*

NP: No, we didn't ask for a censorship visa. In the States they had some problems with the film. A whole story, someone has been sued.

JG: *What happened in 1975 when the film was awarded a prize by the* CNC?

NP: It's a whole story. This was why one of the prints went to Paule Thévenin. It was a misunderstanding. I knew Jean Genet very well – we were 'accomplices'. Before this he would still, as a way of life, make some robberies and things like that. I was connected with that which means I was very close friends with him. When I married he was my 'best man'. He wrote about *Les Abysses* – three or four pages – and about *Les Patres du désordre*. We were very close. So what happened is that, as I said before, we didn't ask for a censorship visa. Now, I know the biggest of the French producers, the President of the Union of Producers, Anatole Dauman. On the liberalisation of censorship he told me, 'You have the rights of Genet's film, why don't we submit it and have it out in the theatres?' So I said, okay let's do it, thinking that there was no problem at all with Genet as I didn't get back the money that I put into the film. We submitted the film as newly done – Anatole Dauman did all that, I wasn't involved; I was making another film at that time, *Gloria Mundi*. He managed to do all this because he was very well known at the CNC. He declared that the film had just been shot now, and everyone knew that it had been shot before. Michel Guy was Minister of Culture by that time – he is homosexual and Genet is homosexual. What happened was that we got the censorship visa, or rather they recognised the film as being done recently and gave some prizes on the character of the film, etc.; all the Commission agreed that the film had been done now and they gave an amount of money to the producer. There was an agreement between Anatole Dauman and me that we would share the prize money if he succeeded in getting it passed as newly done. We got the prize and it was published in the newspapers. Genet got furious because he thought that this prize had been given to him by Michel Guy. He wrote a declaration to the paper that he didn't accept any prize of this, and this, and things like that, which was a kind of personal revenge against Michel Guy, and the whole thing started there. I had to go through suing, the Courts, he took a lawyer about the whole case. I was always being condemned for the whole thing. I told him, 'Listen, what is going on with you? Your philosophy is not to go to the Courts whatever happens'. We did not agree. And it was Paule Thévenin who advised him about the whole thing. So it was a mess. I gave back the money to the CNC and it stopped there. This is the whole story about that. It's sad. We didn't speak any more. He knew that I would have to give back the money and he wanted to give me money. I refused, I said, 'I don't want you to give me money, you've hurt me and damaged our friendship.' I was very sad because he died, and I'd wanted to . . . Maybe I was the closest friend he had outside of his boyfriends, but Paule Thévenin took him. He put himself into the political things. He went close to the Communists and the whole thing was – God! – a mess.

JG: *You own the rights to the film.*

NP: I own them and I own the negative. No print can come out without my permission.

JG: *There's only one print with a distributor in Paris now, and that's the Collectif Jeune Cinéma.*

NP: They don't own the rights. It's illegal.

JG: *The ones in London are legal?*

NP: Yes, I sold the rights. At that time my ex-wife [Anouk Aimée] was married to Albert Finney who had a company, or a friend who had a company, who bought the rights to the film. And Grove Press in the States have the rights.

JG: *Do you know anything about the music track by Gavin Bryars being added to one of the prints in England?*

NP: No. How is the reserve with the music?

JG: *It's very beautiful. Instrumental.*

NP: Does it match with the film?

JG: *Absolutely.*

NP: What happened with Genet's relationship with the film – he didn't recognise the film by the end. He wouldn't consider the film as a good work ever. He refused it. That's why the whole thing happened, because he didn't want the film to come out. He wasn't pleased with that. In the beginning he recognised the film as a good one. But he evolved politically. He thought that socially speaking it was not a good film. Politically, aesthetically, he was not pleased anymore with the film. You can understand that if you really see the film coldly, without thinking it's a film by Jean Genet. It's a very romantic film, a very sentimental film. It's a very SOFT film – a 'fleur bleue', a little romance. It's a love story between two prisoners. One of them dreams that he has this bucolic thing [laughs]. My opinion is that his film was very daring in the beginning when he made it, but things have evolved. In censorship homosexuality is not banned as it was before – it's recognised now. What little remains of the film is the story between two characters, the dream of one who is very much in love with the other and things like that. So you can understand that he wouldn't really like it by the end of his life.

He was very pleased in the beginning, and everybody was, I was very pleased with the reserve too. But things have changed. The last time I saw the film was in England, Albert Finney was there with Anouk, people were there. In my imagination the film was so great and I was very disappointed in seeing it. Disappointed, the meaning of the film had been lowered. Genet had made more powerful works since then, like his plays, such as *Les Nègres*, a fantastic play, it's the play I like most by Genet. This is a more achieved work. If you compare this work, although it is nothing to do with the play, then *Les Nègres* is [up] there and the film is [down] there. It's not that powerful, it's just a romantic story between two prisoners.

Things have evolved. You know if I read some of Genet's books today such as *Notre dame des fleurs*, I think he's a fantastic writer, but I don't have the surprise of the first reading. I discover his technique, it comes out easier. I am more coded to his preoccupations, how he builds his characters. I have less surprise with that. What comes out is the way he has fantastic sentences, but there is always a decorum, an artificiality which is a kind of mannerism coming out. These come out stronger than the inside thing now. Some works remain very strongly, such as *Les Nègres*, but others less so. If you compare (we're coming now to the literature!) the big writers, I don't think that he's a great man. If you compare Céline and him, the one that would remain strong is Céline. Céline admired Genet and Genet admired Céline, because they invented a new kind of writing. But I think that Céline will remain more universally than Genet.

JG: *Returning to the film, was* Un Chant d'amour *the first film that you worked on – as producer or in any way?*

NP: Yes.

JG: *I recently saw Kenneth Anger speaking at the Cinémathèque. He described how he showed* Fireworks *there in 1950 and how Genet was there in the audience, along with Cocteau, Franju ... Comparisons have been made between* Fireworks *and* Un Chant d'amour. *Did Genet ever mention Anger's film?*

NP: I don't know if there's any relationship between the two films; I'm not sure if Genet ever spoke about it.

JG: *In 1950 did you have any filmic influences which you brought to the making of* Un Chant d'amour? *I realise that you were not director or cameraman, but maybe you had some ideas about how the film should look.*

NP: I didn't interfere in any way. But from the beginning of my involvement in the movie business, and all my life, with La Rose Rouge it was the same thing: what I am interested in is to find new things. What does that mean, 'new things'? Not new just for the sake of it, but things that destroy the academies of the past. That's why I was interested in Jean Genet. Every show in La Rose Rouge was a new attempt to find new things. A new approach to screenplays or things like that. I'm always interested in that; my last film was not the same as the one before. It's my craziness. Now, if I do this it means that I'm not much of an admirer of past film-making or an admirer of any movie-maker, because I have to be very strong in myself to hold onto the way I do things. If I start admiring Buñuel or Godard, I'll be close to doing things like Buñuel or Godard. I'm obliged to refuse them, to say I don't like them, or I don't want to know about them. Genet was the same. I gave him the money and he did what he wanted. His life and way of thinking was research into a new kind of writing, a new kind of film-making. He was a poet and tried to invent things all the time, every time he would consider something, and this is what I'm interested in.

JG: *But you have spoken of your admiration for Japanese cinema as a meeting of the natural and the theatrical.*

NP: Two things. One is the word 'admire'. I think that it's an appropriate term in relation to one who sees something and appreciates it. But say I see a painting and it moves me, like a Goya, Greco or Rembrandt. I don't admire it, it MOVES me – it's stronger than admiration. My relation with the painting is very deep, profound. There is no admiration there. 'Admiration' is a term that everybody uses that doesn't mean anything to do with the relationship between the work of art and the feeling for it. [Secondly], with the cinema – it could have gone close to an artistic expression. For me it is an aesthetic expression when it comes close to the theatrical. That means a transposition of the text, of dialogue; a trans-position of the gesture; a transposition of the reality; of the dramaturgy. Mostly in films there is no transposition of the thing, no transposition of the story; they take it as it is. They speak as we speak so everyone can recognise the dialogue. With the gesture it's the same thing, you have to recognise the everyday gesture. People identify with the gesture, they find out it's the same as when they write, or go to the toilet, or something like that. The cinema made is prosaic, it's not poetic, it's not a work of art.

For me to make a kind of allegorical, metaphoric thing – you know the tutu in ballet? There is no tutu in cinema. The cinema would be a work of art if there was more tutu. When you see a ballet you see the tutu and it moves you. Why? It's not realistic, people don't dance in the streets like that. In cinema there is no attempt to move away from the thing. That's my point of view about cinema and why I consider it to be a work of art or not. That's why I like the Japanese cinema, it's BOOM BOOM, WOA WOA, it's beautiful! It's a very new thing, like Noh, where does it come from? It's a complete transposition of life, and that makes it art for me.

JG: *We've talked about how* Un Chant d'amour *was something new and how you reject past films and film-makers as encroaching upon and compromising your originality. In a previous interview you described each of your films as a 'mise-en-cause' [putting into question] of the one before. When you made* Les Abysses *had you carried forward the experience of* Un Chant d'amour?

NP: No. *Les Abysses* was inspired by the same story as *Les Bonnes*. I returned to the real fact to make the scenario. The film and the play therefore could have been close to each other but they are not. You can compare them.

JG: *After* Un Chant d'amour *you co-produced John Cassavetes'* Shadows *in 1959 and then directed* Les Abysses *(1962),* Les Patres du désordre *(1967),* Gloria Mundi *(1975) and* La

Photo *(1987).*

Was Un Chant d'amour *the first film that Genet worked on too?*

NP: Yes, the first and the last.

JG: *Did you know about his work on the project* La Nuit Venue *in the late 70s?*

NP: No, but Genet tried to make money. Maybe he promised and never did it, or he wrote it, got the money and didn't give it to them. Like with *Mademoiselle. Mademoiselle* was a script he wrote and gave to Anouk as a marriage gift. [Laughs] One day somebody asked him if he wanted to sell the scenario and he sold it for a high price without even telling her!

JG: *Have you had some success with* La Photo?

NP: It was in Cannes Festival.

My problem was, it's a very strange film. For me it's a new way of making a film. I was wondering if it would work as a show for an audience as there are no conflictual situations in the film – no oppositions like in my other films. There are two characters only, like [*Sleuth*]. I mention this film because of its thriller elements, both are in the same house, there was a murder, one of them wanted to make the other … but this film, there is no police element in it, no enquiry. The film functions like a thriller, there's an angle coming out, without all these dramatic elements which are in them. It was a challenge to make a film like that, and it works fine.

JG: *Are you ever satisfied with your work, or are you always thinking about the next project?*

NP: I'm not very pleased about the film. If you make a challenge, say 'I will try to do that to find out if it works', when it works I have a kind of satisfaction. Not for the achievement of the film, that you have to refuse, but to find out it works and to go on to try new things every time. The problem with cinema is that nobody dares try.

JG: *Are you unhappy with the film* Gloria Mundi?

NP: It's not the fact that I'm not happy. The film is about torture. All kinds of torture, one of the ideas being a power relationship between two people. Always torture in a relationship, between son and mother or whatever, there is a relationship of one being weaker than the other, which I tried to film. Also political torture. There were scenes in the film – a true story – about an Algerian terrorist who had been raped by a French officer with a bottle of beer. He tortured her in front of her father. So there's a scene like that in the film. When I was making the film I said to myself, I will succeed in making a film about torture if the audience does not identify themselves with the film, if the audience refuses the film. If they don't refuse it and they accept the film then I have failed. And that's exactly what happened. It was a kind of suicide as a movie-maker. I thought that I would never make another film. So many things were involved in it. I don't think of it in that sense, as a good or bad film; it's not a film for me. The film hasn't been accepted and of course I'm pleased about that but at the same time it's a negative situation. It was a film. When you make a film you make it for an audience or you don't make it. I made a film NOT for the audience which is a very contradictory thing. But I think this was the only way of doing it, of dealing with torture. This was the contradiction of the film.

Appendix II

Notes on Filming *Le Bagne*[1]

Written in the early 1950s after the success of *Un Chant d'amour*, Genet's film script *Le Bagne* (The Penal Colony) features notes on casting, technique, and his views on the facility and the specific potential of the medium of cinema:

> *I have a few stipulations for the way in which it is to be filmed. The close-ups should be very dark. No close-ups of faces, but those of gestures, which without the immodesty of the camera would stay unseen … In a certain situation, a clenched fist can move us enormously, if the eye registers the texture of the skin, a black nail here, a wart, and the furtive caress of a finger on the palm that we wouldn't have seen at the theatre, for example – and perhaps which the characters ignore. In effect the cinema is basically immodest. Let us use this facility to enlarge gestures. The camera can open a fly and search out its secrets …[2]*

> *The enlarged appearance of a ball of saliva in the corner of a mouth can, as the scene unfolds, arouse an emotion in the viewer which would give a weight, a new depth to this drama.[3]*

Notes

1. Unpublished. 195?. Translated by Stuart Burleigh, 1990.

2. *Le Bagne* p. 12.

3. *Le Bagne* p. 13.

Appendix III

Notes for the Production Of *La Nuit venue/Le Bleu de l'oeil* (The Night Has Come/The Blue of the Eye)

I believe that the colour green should dominate. Different greens on the door, as if it had been repainted several times.

The graffiti is in red, some is in black, more is scratched into the wood.

Find and reproduce graffiti from real toilets, or drawings by mad people (ask at the Saint-Anne Hospital).

✳

The walls of the toilet are made of white earthenware with green blotches.

Well in view: the cistern and chain of the toilet.

Also well in view: a wad of torn up newspaper on a string to the right side of the toilet.

✳

The inspector, bending, with his cap well back on his head down towards his neck and his tunic unbuttoned.

✳

When the inspector straightens himself up, he buttons his trousers and tunic.

We see that he is wearing a strapping and well cut uniform.

The two old Arabs – with white beards of five or six days' growth – are very childlike, laughable, two street arabs.

✻

All the leaves of the trees in the square have fallen.

On the ground, dead leaves of all colours.

✻

The earth of the square: white.

Black pigeons.

✻

In the distance there are silhouettes. Two or three of which are dressed as women – one with a parasol and train, despite the night. The women are much bigger than the men.

✻

The train of A.'s costume, which was very neat, is already creased and stained.

✻

A. can already see the town; she re-experiences the emotions provoked by what happened with the inspector.

Hence: the white cop and the Black man are bigger than life (nearly on stilts). The face and hands of the Black man are gilded.

✻

It would be good for there to be a full moon over the Louvre.

✻

Even at night the cops would have white gloves and red epaulettes.

✢

Under the vault of the Carousel arch.

The down and outs and beggars are in the vault, out of the way. As water floods over the ground they move up to the vault to protect themselves.

They clutch themselves like bats. They are grey (clothes and faces) with touches of red, yellow, green.

The police beat: five policemen enter through the arch.

A cop shines his torch towards the ceiling. He exchanges a wink with a beggar.

✢

Emphasise the creole accent and the amused air of the black priests.

Even the one with white hair.

Use actors who have very visible whites of the eyes in the black of the night.

✢

It's a circus scene where the nurses play a game with the beds on wheels. They push them, and push them again, by hand or foot.

In the chariot-beds you can see the deathly pale faces and the panic-stricken looks of the dying. They are all white, even more than white: transparent.

Don't make-up the actors who play the sick, but simply paint their faces with ivory Valentine paint. Two or three brush strokes without forgetting the lips, and a few hairs poking out of the nightcaps for the old men and women.

This scene must be accompanied by the aria of 'Sancta Maria' by Monteverdi in the background.

The scraps of this scene will be incorporated in the images to come.

*

I believe that it needs a wall which is very black, as if tarred, to make the yellow of the oranges stand out.

If possible the ground would be blackened when the oranges roll on the earth.

*

I believe that the facade of the brothel should be ROSE coloured (with beams).

Costumes of arab workers in the line: black – a lot of black – green, yellow – indigo blue.

*

The girl who offers sweets is covered in cheap and nasty jewellery.

*

The Black's trousers are made of silk or moire, tight fitting; black patent shoes.

⁎

The stairs. Seen from above.

Blacks at each window. And bamboo canes which hold up lighted Chinese lanterns.

Painted stairway.

Transvestites all along the stairway.

Seven guitar players on the left hand side.

The wedding party is sumptuously dressed.

The bride's train, made of silk with a violet lining, is three metres long. Veil of tulle.

A tiara. The groom has long blonde hair.

⁎

The wedding must be taken in from top to bottom.

⁎

One must have the impression that the shadows seen in the beginning (in Paris), in the gardens of the Tuileries, have become real beings: women bigger than men.

Notes

1. First published in *Camera/Stylo* (France) no. 4, September 1983, pp. 89–91. Translated by Stuart Burleigh, 1990.

Appendix IV

The Cinema of Saint Genet

The following films, which are in chronological order, constitute a National Film Theatre Season (April 1991) entitled 'The Cinema of Saint Genet'. The films are either written or directed by Genet, adapt his writings, influence or are influenced by his work or feature an appearance by him. Titles unavailable for the season are indicated by an asterisk.

1947: *Fireworks*
(Kenneth Anger, USA, 14 mins)
Anger claims that Genet saw *Fireworks* in 1950. Probable influence on *Un Chant d'amour*.

Ulysse

*1948: *Ulysse (Les Mauvaises Rencontres)*
(Alexandre Astruc, France, 90 mins)
From the novel *Cette sacrée salade* by Cecil Saint-Laurent. Reported appearance by Genet.

1950: *Un Chant d'amour*
(Jean Genet, France, 25 mins)

sc; supervising ed: Jean Genet; p: Nico Papatakis; ph: Jacques Natteau; lp: Lucien Sénemaud (younger convict), Java (whose hand swings the blossom), Coco Le Martiniquais (dancing African prisoner), André Reybaz (stand-in).

*1950: *Untitled*

3-minute home movie with Violette Leduc.

1955: *Goubbiah (Kiss Of Fire)*

(Robert Darene, France, 95 mins)

From the novel by Jean Mantet. Includes some dialogue written by Genet.

1962: *Les Abysses*

(Nico Papatakis, France, 96 mins)

Version of the same events depicted in *Les Bonnes* and the first film directed by the producer of *Un Chant d'amour*.

*1962: *Arrestation d'un tireur des toits*

(Pierre Grimblat, France, ? mins)

An adaptation of *Pompes funèbres* that was never commercially released. Genet requested that his name be removed from the credits.

1962: *The Balcony*

(Joseph Strick, USA, 86 mins)
Adaptation of Genet's play
Le Balcon.

The Balcony

1965: *Deathwatch*

    (Vic Morrow, USA, 88 mins)

    Adaptation of Genet's play *Haute Surveillance*.

1966: *Mademoiselle*

    (Tony Richardson, GB, 103 mins)

    From Genet's filmscript *Les Rêves interdits, ou, l'autre versant du rêve*.

Mademoiselle

Possession du condamné

1967: *La Possession du condamné*

    (Albert-André Lheureux, Belgium, 14 mins)

    An adaptation of Genet's poem 'Le Condamné à mort' (The Man Condemned to Death).

1969: *Prologue*

    (Robin Spry, Canada, 88 mins)

    Appearance by Genet.

1974: *The Maids*

    (Christopher Miles, GB, 95 mins)

    Adaptation of Genet's play *Les Bonnes*.

1981: *Genet*

>(Antoine Bourseiller, France, 60 mins)
>Documentary on Genet.

1982: *Querelle – Ein Pakt mit dem Teufel*

>(Rainer Werner Fassbinder, West Germany, 108 mins)
>Adaptation of Genet's novel *Querelle de Brest*.

1985: *Saint Genet*

>(Nigel Williams/Charles Chabot, GB, 60 mins)
>BBC Arena documentary.

1985: *Le Sphinx*

>(Thierry Knauss, France, 12 mins)
>Adaptation of Genet's text 'Four Hours at Chatila'.

1986: *Jean Genet is Dead*

>(Constantin Giannaris, GB, 25 mins)
>Inspired by Genet's novel *Journal du voleur*.

1987: *Miracle of the Rose*

>(Cerith Wyn Evans, GB, 23 mins)
>Inspired by Genet's novel *Miracle de la rose*.

1988: *The Ballad of Reading Gaol*

>(Richard Kwietniowski, GB, 12 mins)
>Inspired in part by *Un Chant d'amour*.

1989: *Ecce Homo*

>(Jerry Tartaglia, USA, 7 mins)
>Optically printed footage from
>*Un Chant d'amour*.

The Ballad of Reading Gaol

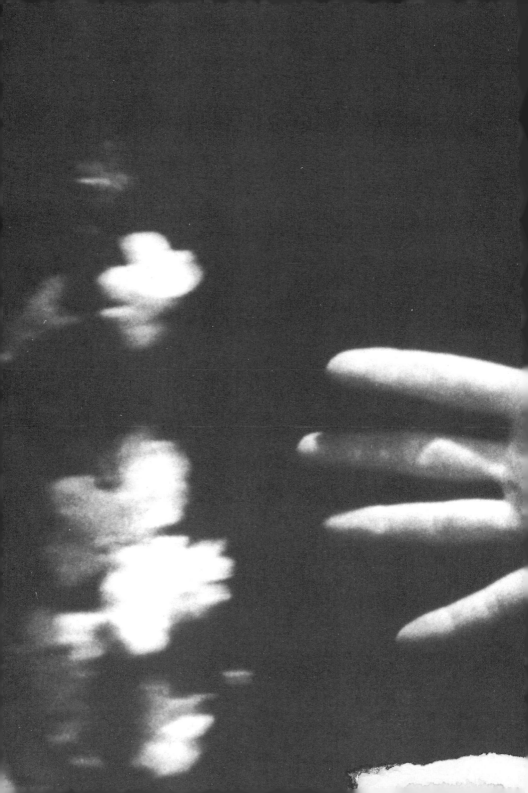